❖ ❖ ❖ ❖ ❖

THE POLITICS OF PUBLIC MEMORY

SUNY Series in Oral and Public History
Michael Frisch, Editor

SUNY Series in Advances in Applied Anthropology
Erve Chambers, Editor

❖ ❖ ❖ ❖ ❖

❖ ❖ ❖ ❖ ❖ ❖ ❖ ❖ ❖ ❖ ❖ ❖ ❖ ❖ ❖

THE POLITICS
OF PUBLIC MEMORY

*Tourism, History, and Ethnicity
in Monterey, California*

Martha K. Norkunas

STATE UNIVERSITY OF NEW YORK PRESS

❖ ❖ ❖ ❖ ❖ ❖ ❖ ❖ ❖ ❖ ❖ ❖ ❖ ❖

Published by
State University of New York Press, Albany

© 1993 State University of New York

For information, address the State University of New York Press,
90 State Street, Suite 700, Albany, NY 12207

Production by Cathleen Collins
Marketing by Theresa A. Swierzowski

Library of Congress Cataloging-in-Publication Data

Norkunas, Martha K.
    The politics of public memory : tourism, history, and
ethnicity in Monterey, California / by Martha K. Norkunas.
      p. cm. — (SUNY series in oral and public history) (SUNY
series in advances in applied anthropology)
    Includes bibliographical references and index.
    ISBN 0–7914–1483–3 — ISBN 0–7914–1484–1 (pbk.)
    1. Tourist trade — Social aspects — California — Monterey.
I. Title. II. Series III. Series : SUNY series in advances in
applied anthropology.
G155.U6N83   1993
979.4'76—dc20   92–42168
                                                 CIP

10 9 8 7 6 5 4 3 2 1

For my family:
Yildiray, Jasmine, Ayla, Emre and Mum

CONTENTS

❖ ❖ ❖ ❖ ❖

ILLUSTRATIONS

❖　❖　❖　❖　❖

Illustrations

ACKNOWLEDGMENTS

❖   ❖   ❖   ❖   ❖

Many people were particularly helpful in the research and writing of this manuscript and I would like to take a moment and acknowledge their contributions.

In Lowell, Massachusetts, special thanks go to Bob Weible and Marty Blatt, two public historians who have had a great impact on my thinking about history. Thanks also to Jim Higgins of Higgins and Ross for developing the cover photograph for this book. In Berkeley, California I owe a debt of gratitude to James Deetz, Alan Dundes, Nelson Graburn, Jane Bendix and the late Reinhard Bendix. Others who lectured at Berkeley were also of special assistance, particularly Roger Abrahams and Dean MacCannell. I was later able to invite Dean MacCannell and John Dorst to speak at a conference in Lowell where we had a wonderful exchange of ideas. There were a number of people who participated in my research in Monterey including Donna Penwell, Carol Chorbajian, Rich Hughett, James Wright, Jonathan Williams, Michael Hemp, Steve Henderson, Joan Pees, Robert Reese, Rudi Hartmann, Peter Coniglio, Nino Palma, Bruce Kibby, and the interpreters at the Monterey State Historic Park. Stephanie Alldredge took slides of many of my sites, and Robin Winslow accompanied me on a number of informal interviews.

Several people read and commented upon drafts of this manuscript. Sandy Stahl, John Bodnar and Ruth Stone offered helpful comments. Richard Bauman provided comments as well as pivotal articles and much encouragement. Michael Frisch read an earlier version of this book and encouraged me to pursue it; his later comments helped me to rethink the structure of these essays. Regina Bendix also took the time to read portions of this manuscript. At the State University of New York Press Rosalie Robertson intelligently and cheerfully guided me through the editorial process, and Cathleen Collins offered many help-ful stylistic suggestions. The anonymous readers for SUNY Press wrote detailed and insightful comments which helped me a great deal in rewriting portions of this manuscript.

Grateful acknowledgment goes to the California Historical Society for granting me permission to quote from "The Larkin House Revis-ited" by Harold Kirker, *California History* LXV:26–33, 73–74; to the Western Tanager Press for granting me permission to quote from *A History of Steinbeck's Cannery Row* by Tom Mangelsdorf; to the Univer-sity of Pennsylvania Press for granting me permission to quote from *The Written Suburb* by John Dorst; and to Harper Collins for granting me permission to quote from *Women, Art and Power* by Linda Nochlin.

I would like to recognize two groups of people who have helped to sensitize me to the need to tell the story of the ethnic past. First are the many people with strong ethnic identities who have allowed me to interview them and who have thoughtfully and articulately told me something of their life stories. It is through them that I have learned how important and how deeply moving is the history of ordinary peo-ple. Secondly are those colleagues, academics and public sector folk-lorists and historians, who struggle to go beyond the history of elite white men. By listening and working to re-present the viewpoints of minorities and the nonelite they are offering new and provocative interpretations of the past.

Finally I would like to say thank you to five people who did not actu-ally help me to write this book but who helped with everything else, especially the inspiration. Our three young children, Jasmine, Ayla and Emre, have taught me a great deal about being forthright, being sensi-tive to the world around us and having a boundless passion for learn-ing. My mother gave me her drive and her determination. She is now teaching me about courage, as she begins her battle with cancer. Yildiray Erdener, my husband, has been an intellectual inspiration to me, a friend, and absolutely the staunchest supporter of my career. He provided me with the space and time to finish this book. They are my family, the wonderful context within which I think and write.

Introduction:
An Intellectual Journey
to the Politics of Culture

❖ ❖ ❖ ❖ ❖

From Authenticity to Cultural Text

Intellectuals are fascinated with the way cultural groups think, behave, create, and express themselves. This kind of institutional empathy was originally what led many of us to enter fields such as folklore, anthropology, sociology, public history, or even journalism. We strive to make, if only for a moment, the self appear strange and the other appear familiar. Our research takes us into these other groups, which sometimes necessitates travel to faraway places, and sometimes brings us only as far as the "foreign" groups living in our own cities. We are in a sense tourists who linger, who pause to dig deeper, to understand more, and to articulate the meaningful patterns we believe are there. If we are entertained in the process, so much the better, but it is the understanding that draws and not the promise of pleasure.

Over the course of the last twenty years, those who engage in what may be called academic tourism have also become increasingly interested in the nonacademic tourist—those who wander for the sake of pleasure or self-fulfillment—and the whole topic of tourism generally. It is fertile ground, for it allows intellectuals to look at the intersections of ethnicity, public history, ritual, pagentry, expressive culture, museum studies, and the politics of memory.

I first became seriously interested in tourism as an academic topic when, in the summer of 1986, I came upon the work of anthropologist Nelson Graburn in *Hosts and Guests* (Smith 1977). Graburn described tourism as a journey from the profane into the sacred and the tourist as being in a symbolically altered state. He wrote from the point of view of

1

the tourist, hypothesizing about what it was like to be a person on a quest for an experience of renewal.

I turned then to other anthropological and sociological literature on tourism. I read several important collections by anthropologists about tourism which appeared in the 1970s and 1980s including *The Anthropology of Tourism* (Graburn 1983) and *Hosts and Guests* (Smith 1977); in addition I looked through the journal devoted to the study of anthropology, sociology, and tourism, *The Annals of Tourism Research.*

A growing number of scholars had turned their attention to the tourist's experience, his or her motivation for travel, and the issue of authenticity at the tourist site. Eric Cohen was most concerned with investigating the relationship between tourists' motivations and the authenticity of their travel experiences (Cohen 1972, 1973, 1974, 1979a, 1979b). Dean MacCannell (1973, 1976, 1984), Philip Pearce and Gianno Moscardo (1986a) were also engaged in analyses of the tourist's encounters with authenticity and with a definition of the term itself.

MacCannell's 1976 work *The Tourist* was one of the first semiotic analyses of the tourist site and the tourist's experience of that site. MacCannell described the tourist as part of a middle class that is striving to transcend the discontinuity of modernity. The postindustrial world engendered feelings of alienation and loss of soul. In this atmosphere, tourism had absorbed some of the social functions of religion as it became an essentially religious quest for authenticity. The tourist seeks to see life as it really is, to get in touch with the natives, to enter the intimate space of the other in order to have an experience of real life, an authentic experience.[1] Yet tourism ends up by promoting the preservation of fictional re-creations of ethnicity as expressions of ethnicity became commodities to be bought and sold. Village life becomes something to see in the recreational repertoire of the tourist rather than a complex of real social activity. Thus modern mass tourism is involved in an important contradiction: it is based on both the international homogenization of the culture of the tourist and the artificial preservation of local ethnic peoples and attractions (MacCannell 1976, 1984).

Several other thinkers reflected upon tourism, authenticity, and ethnicity in a special issue of *The Annals of Tourism Research* entitled "Tourism and Ethnicity" (Van den Berghe and Keyes 1984). The collection examines the impact of ethnic tourism upon the ethnic him or herself and the ramifications of offering up local culture for sale. The role the natives often play, as part of the show the tourist comes to see, engenders a special kind of ethnic interaction between themselves and the tourists. The irony is that the presence of tourists, whose whole experience depends on the authenticity of what is presented to them, spoils the natives by making them less exotic and more like the tourists themselves, and eventually causes the natives to transform their behavior according to the perceived tastes of the tourist (1984:346). Such "bastardized" versions of the natives' cultural heritage may become, for the native, "authentic" markers of a re-created identity. The natives' own identity, changed to suit what are believed to be tourists' tastes, becomes so known and so ingrained, and perhaps encouraged by developers and the state, that it eventually becomes accepted as true by the natives themselves.

One very special work, Lionel Trilling's *Sincerity and Authenticity* (1971), treated the history and literature of authenticity. As a folklorist I was interested in the relationship between folklore and authenticity. This brought me to Richard Dorson's fakelore essays (1950, 1969, 1982), and the work of Hermann Bausinger (1986), Regina Bendix (1988), Linda Dégh (1977/78), and Allen Dundes (1985), who all grappled with defining the limits of genuine folklore.

Meanwhile, I spent two blocks of time, for a total of twenty months, living with my family in Monterey, California. During my initial stay I played the roles of resident and tourist. Just as folklorists are ethnographic tourists, tourists, as Dean MacCannell pointed out, are "ethnographers of modernity" and so, in that sense, I had begun my fieldwork informally long before I began it in a serious, concentrated way (MacCannell 1976). Initially I lived quite close to one of the major tourist areas in Monterey, Cannery Row, and later lived just above a second tourist destination, Fisherman's Wharf. From time to time I did some temporary work in offices in Salinas, Pacific Grove, and Monterey and taught at Monterey Peninsula College, the local community college. At the same time I was an insider—a resident of Monterey and a worker on the Peninsula—and an outsider—a long-term tourist, new to the area, curious about it, an observer rather than a full participant in the local culture.

I spent the next nine months in the library at the University of California at Berkeley reading about tourism. When I returned to Monterey I became a hyper-tourist, swallowing up whatever was available to see and to experience. My goal was to assume the roles of each of the many kinds of tourists who came to the area and to see and do what they would see and do. While I went on commercial and nonprofit tours and interviewed tour industry owners, tour operators, Monterey State Historic Park tour guides, the State Park historian, museum directors, shop and restaurant owners, ethnic community leaders, foundation directors, and corporate developers, most of my time was spent at the tourist sites as an observer.

Gradually it became clear to me that while the literature on authenticity was applicable to those tourist areas in Monterey that treated the presentation of the past as history, it alone did not serve to interpret the more commercial tourist areas in the city. I knew I needed a different kind of approach to come to an understanding of my sites individually and collectively. Much of what I had been reading focused on the meaning of the tourist experience for the tourist or guest. What I had become intrigued by in Monterey was the opposite perspective: that of the site itself, or host. I wondered what messages the host was communicating about its past, its present identity, its values and its ideology.

During this period I had the good fortune to talk to Jim Deetz about my research. He handed me an article by Mark Leone and another by Alison Wylie that analyzed the implicit messages communicated by particular museum presentations (Leone 1981, 1981a; Wylie 1985). Later I met Mark Leone, who referred me to Richard Handler's *Nationalism and the Politics of Culture in Quebec* (1988). I had entered the world of public history and historic preservation and found certain other works to be equally as provocative: Charles Hosmer's 1965 study of the American preservation movement, and Michael Wallace's powerful critiques of history museums (1986), industrial museums (1987), and Disneyland (1989). Wallace looked at the presentation of the past in terms of the new social history: How had the lives of ordinary people been presented? How had ideas about class and power relationships been treated by museums? In the new era of postindustrialism, how was the topic of industrial capitalism examined?

What I came to understand about my own research was that I was dealing not only with the construction of public culture, but the creation of value. Richard Bauman introduced me to the work of Michael Thompson, whose *Rubbish Theory* (1979) examined the social creation of value. I later came upon an insightful critique of tourism by John Dorst (Dorst 1989), who applied theories of postmodernity to Chadds Ford, Pennsylvania. I considered the work of folklorists and historians who had also turned their attention to a political critique of museum displays (Schlereth 1985, 1990; Leon and Rosenzweig 1989).

Museums were, I then saw, but one part of this effort—one part of the tourist experience. Each of the different tourist landscapes in Monterey, whether they are historic or commercial, could be read as distinct cultural texts. I began to think of the whole tourist environment as a cultural production, a kind of outdoor museum displaying the artifacts of society, a collection of cultural texts. I sought to describe and analyze Monterey's cultural texts of tourism and finally to examine the ideological assumptions underlying the tourist environment as a cultural production.

The Politics of History

Certain books and articles had led me to think about how distinct tourist sites functioned as systems. The entire system was built upon a selective reinterpretation of the past. I began to think about the remarkable study, *The Invention of Tradition* (Hobsbawm and Ranger 1983), which questioned the creation and political uses of a number of cherished traditions. These traditions were actually "invented traditions" that had become legitimate through repetition, or a process of formalization and ritualization characterized by reference to the past. Through this implied continuity with the past, these "traditions" acted to inculcate certain values and norms of behavior. The invention of tradition occurred most frequently in times of social change (Hobsbawn and Ranger 1983:1–5). The result was that

> the history which became part of the fund of knowledge or the ideology of nation, state or movement is not what has actually been preserved in popular memory, but what has been selected, written, pictured, popularized and institutionalized by those whose function it is to do so (Hobsbawm 1983:13).[2]

The public would accept as "true" history that is written, exhibited, or otherwise publicly sanctioned. What is often less obvious to the public is that the writing or the exhibition itself is reflective of a particular ideology.[3] In an editorial in the *Archaeological Bulletin*, John Parkington and Andrew Smith observed that archaeology, like museum exhibits and tourist sites, is not a past revealed but a new construction of a cultural past.

> The past, as promoted by archaeologists, or historians for that matter, is not reconstructed but constructed, that archaeological facts, far from

speaking for themselves, are created and marshalled consciously or sub-
consciously by archaeologists for a variety of purposes (1986:43).

If the past is created, it is evidently done so in the present to legitimize
contemporary personal, social, and political circumstances. Archaeology
and anthropology offer pointed examples. Born in the era of European
colonialism, archaeology and anthropology described non-European
peoples as primitive or childlike in order to justify political domination
by more "civilized" peoples in the name of progress (see Parkington and
Smith 1986:43; see also Finnegan 1969). This reconstruction is done
through a series of subtle distortions: the simplification of imagery, the
obfuscation of historical complexities and discontinuities, the reinforce-
ment of stereotypes, and the presentation of history as natural and
inevitable.

Monuments and historical sites, meant to symbolize complex move-
ments or historical events, could instead act to enshrine singular visions
of the past. The Statue of Liberty and its accompanying poem, for
example, provided an "instant and popular interpretation of the immigrant movement," which not only threatened to turn historical reality
into a cliché by explaining all immigrant experience in terms of a quest
for freedom, but preempted any other possible explanations of the
complexity of immigration. Symbolic history was enacted at the
expense of actual history in the shadow of the Statue (Bodnar 1986:
137–43, 147).

In describing the American experience in Vietnam, Frances Fitzgerald wrote that the United States was not just traveling to another country, it was entering another cultural landscape. It became increasingly
difficult for Americans to understand the impossibility of transposing
their values and way of life onto a culture so radically different from
their own (Fitzgerald 1972). In a similar vein, David Lowenthal entitled
his reflections on historic preservation *The Past is a Foreign Country*.
Like travel to another land, travel to the past involves recognition of a
cultural landscape based on premises different from our own. The
impulse is to remake the past based on contemporary images: the faults
of Washington and Jefferson are downplayed, for example, while those
qualities that are esteemed today are highlighted. Our contemporary
depictions of Washington and Jefferson conceal their faults so that
their "greatness" obscures their actual eighteenth century conduct as
slaveholders (Lowenthal 1985: xxiv, 343).

In his discussion of the reconstruction of Shakertown, Mark Leone noted that the presentation involves the museum's systematic fragmentation of Shaker culture in such a way that it ultimately trivializes those aspects of Shaker life that deviate from our own. Shaker culture is made to stand not as a social experiment dedicated to resolving or escaping the repressive conditions of emergent industrial capitalism, but as an object lesson warning against departure from the norms that structure life in the modern industrial capitalist world (Leone 1981:305–8; Wylie 1985:139). In fact, utopian ventures as a whole, which constitute an inordinately large proportion of American outdoor history museums, are never adequately portrayed in twentieth century restorations of their lifestyles. "More often than not, the once bitterly maligned countercultures of earlier eras have been homogenized into respectable middle-class cultural establishments" (Schlereth 1990:352).

I reflected back upon MacCannell's idea that the postmodern world had engendered a loss of soul, a feeling of alienation, and that tourism had supplanted certain religious functions. Perhaps, I mused, we were involved in an important moment of social change, in which Hobsbawm and Ranger had predicted new traditions would be invented. Certainly we no longer based our economy on the production of goods and we were desperately searching for a new economic base. A whole series of relationships was shifting and I sensed a desperate need to reaffirm certain ideologies and class relationships that would no longer be valid as the social order changed. This was being done through certain museum installations that were representing the past to legitimate a disappearing present.

The problems associated with ethnic tourism in which indigenous peoples began to shape their cultural identities according to what they believed tourists wanted to see had been well articulated. This was a kind of participation in stereotyping, a tacit agreement to domination. The changed identity becomes accepted as true by the native him or herself. This could happen historically as well as culturally, as when the "natives'" role in the past was altered to the point that they themselves came to believe that the selected history was their actual history. Alternatively, references to ethnic groups could be so removed from the tourist landscape as to be a denial that those groups existed in the past or in the present.

The reconstruction of the past, and the reinterpretation of the present is not confined to a museum or monument setting. Public culture is constructed on many different levels, including tourism, but its common denominator is that it stands as a series of texts that can be read by the general public. Each of these texts has qualities peculiar unto itself, yet all share a set of assumptions about the world. In Monterey the texts concern a set of assumptions about dominance, class, ethnicity, nature, history, the literary landscape, economics as played out in the transformation from industrialism to postindustrialism, and the public construction of culture as tourism. These assumptions reflect the ideology of their creators, and hence the reader of the texts is lead to the notion of hegemony.

What the public is reading in Monterey are hegemonic texts reflective of a particular ideology that legitimates the current social structure. This structure involves several ideas: that those of middle- and upper middle-class, white European descent are naturally and logically in power as the result of the forward linear movement of history, and that contemporary relationships of power and domination are justified in social evolutionary terms. The tourists and locals who participate in this tourist environment effectively consent to this symbolic domination. This scenario is created and recreated throughout the museum and commercial tourist areas of Monterey. It is created by a white, upper middle-class audience (members of historical societies and tourism promoters) for a middle-class audience (tourists to the area). Through repeated references to an extremely selective past, traditions are invented and values reified. This kind of social Darwinism applies as well to nature as it does to ethnicity and class. Dominance as an idea is extended to nature, as wild fish and fowl appear as subordinates performing for the pleasure of tourists.

There are and have always been social critics who attack this particular construction of public culture. One important critic was John Steinbeck, who glorified some of the very social classes and ethnic groups who had been excised from the present and the image of the past. The response to his literature became, in turn, part of the complex series of cultural texts in the tourist landscape. His critique of the powerful was rendered impotent as his ideas were transformed into literary caricatures. His fiction, an art form that was based upon reality, initially came to represent that reality. Gradually his literature was transformed into a more socially palatable tale, as his heroes and heroines were changed into humorous caricatures of their former selves. Thus, commercial tourist developers had altered fiction, which itself had come to represent a historical epoch in the city's industrial past. History, literature, industrialism, nature, and dominance all intersect in the tourist landscape in Monterey.

In the chapters that follow, I discuss in detail the typologies at work in the public culture of Monterey, California. I look at a moment in time in the city, a moment ripe with large scale social and economic changes. Monterey is a small seaside community (population approximately 30,000) on the Monterey Peninsula, located 120 miles south of San Francisco. While several of the Peninsula cities (Monterey, Carmel, Pacific Grove, and Pebble Beach) are marketed as a tourist package, each community has its own specific tourist sites. In Monterey I identified three distinct tourist sites: the Path of History, a series of historic houses that winds through "old" Monterey; Cannery Row, the street where Monterey's sardine canneries once flourished and which is the subject of John Steinbeck's novel of the same name; and Fisherman's Wharf, a former fishing pier now filled with shops and restaurants.

The first chapter is primarily descriptive. It sets the general context for the analyses that follow, by describing Monterey in ethnographic and historical terms.

Chapter Two is a specific examination of the politics of history and the ideology embedded in a historical construct. I look at a selectively reconstructed history represented by upper-class homes and socially elite societies. My analysis is based upon the Path of History that purports to tell the history of the city.

Chapter Three builds upon the notion of a selectively reconstructed history as I examine the relationships between history, economics, nature, and the literary landscape. Cannery Row, once the site of industrial canneries packing sardines, is today a commercial tourist site that bases its marketing plan upon references to history, nature, and literature. The way that these elements are manipulated in this public context helps to further illuminate the ideological assumptions underlying the whole system of tourism in Monterey.

Chapter Four once again draws upon the presentation of the past as well as upon ideas of nature portrayed in the public texts. This time ethnic references are more explicitly examined as they appear upon the landscape in the form of ethnic monuments and statuary. The site for the analysis is Fisherman's Wharf.

Finally, I use the conclusion to round out my argument, referencing the data I have discussed in the body of this work.

By acting as an "ethnographer of modernity" I have tried to articulate how one community has used public history and tourism to communicate specific ideas about power relationships. This is then a modern ethnography of the powerful and the powerless and of how the ideology of the powerful is systematically embedded in the institutions and public texts of tourism and history. My analysis is rooted in description. It is my hope that the issues I have raised through the Monterey example will prove fruitful to those instrumental in constructing other public cultural landscapes.

Notes

1. In between an authentic experience and one that is completely fabricated are what MacCannell called "staged authenticity" or areas that the tourist establishment construct to appear more like something actual (a look *inside*) which gives the tourist the impression of having had an authentic experience (MacCannell 1976).
2. This is a well-known fact in African Studies, where research on genealogists has found that they "remember" the past according to the political exigencies of the present. For examples, see Finnegan 1969.
3. As Edward Countryman wrote, any reconstruction of the past, whether academic or fictional, becomes itself a cultural artifact, a reflection of its time (Countryman 1986:87).

1

❖   ❖   ❖

Ethnography and History:
The Monterey Example

❖   ❖   ❖   ❖   ❖

Monterey: A Contemporary Perspective

Monterey, California, is one component in a system of tourist sites which includes Seventeen Mile Drive, Pebble Beach, Carmel and Pacific Grove. The Peninsula is an entire "package" that is sold to tourists, although some come specifically to golf at Pebble Beach, while conventioneers rarely stray outside of Monterey proper. People are drawn to the area because of the climate, the scenic rocky coastline, the many state parks and campsites in the area, the beaches, forests, golf courses, shops, and restaurants. Some also come to the area to see the landscapes that inspired international literary figures such as John Steinbeck, Robert Louis Stevenson, and the many other artists, writers, and poets who lived or live on the Peninsula.

The vivid beauty of the natural landscape is evident everywhere along those sections of coastline that have not been developed. Some areas, such as Pebble Beach and Pacific Grove, took special pains to create and maintain a scenic coastal road, and whether one walks along the pedestrian paths in Pacific Grove or drives the scenic route, the ocean and the rocky shores are very beautiful and very visible. Monterey, on the other hand, devoted itself to more obvious commercial interests. This resulted in car dealerships and other business structures being built adjacent to the ocean, effectively blocking any view of the

Fig. 1–1. Monterey Bay and Fisherman's Wharf (photo by M. Norkunas 1987).

sea from the major avenue in town (Del Monte Avenue). As the city struggles to move completely away from an economy based on manufacturing to one based on service, it has begun to buy up the leases of these businesses. The city plans to create a "Window on the Bay," opening up a vista of the shoreline.

While lawns are not a common sight, flower and fruit trees line residential streets. Many residents keep small gardens, for the climate of the area is very mild. In the Portuguese sections of the city, grape arbors are common. Winter sees no snow but much rain. Fog rolls into the Peninsula every morning, but by midday, in the spring, summer, and fall, it has been burnt away by the temperate sun. The average annual temperature is fifty-six degrees. In the summer months the temperature reaches the sixties and, on occasion, hits the seventies but rarely goes higher, while in winter it can become cold but never freezes.

As in the past, the contemporary Monterey Peninsula is an ethnically and economically stratified area. Multimillion dollar estates line Seventeen Mile Drive as it winds its way through Pebble Beach and into Carmel. Carmel and Carmel Valley are upper middle-class towns, boasting literary figures, movie stars, and high real estate prices. Pacific Grove and Monterey are more residential areas, offering housing to professional people, to the international staff of the Defense Language Institute (DLI is a military language school teaching more than forty-four languages and dialects), to military personnel from DLI and from Fort Ord, to the many retired people who move to the area, to shop owners, and to the waitresses and store employees, bookkeepers and administrators who are employed by the tourist and local businesses.

Seaside, Sand City, and Marina are for insiders and are not highlighted as tourist areas. While these cities have middle-class housing, they are known on the Peninsula as being "tough places to live." Most of the working classes and minority groups on the Peninsula live in these cities, with Seaside housing a significant African-American population. While some Mexican-Americans live in these three towns, most reside in the agricultural areas located west of Monterey.

The major industry on the Peninsula through the 1980s has been the military, due to the presence of the Fort Ord Army Base, the Naval Post Graduate School, and the Defense Language Institute. The second largest industry is tourism. Some Peninsula cities make a major effort to create and control the tourist environment. The city of Carmel, for example, maintains strict control over shop signs, as well as over the kinds of artifacts one may sell in any given store. One florist was denied a permit to sell flower vases that the city's governing board deemed to be of insufficient quality and, hence, smacking of souvenir status. This tight control over artifacts and building facades was one of the major issues leading to the election of Clint Eastwood as mayor of Carmel in the mid-1980s. Eastwood's election, in turn, heightened the tourist traffic to Carmel, and his own Hog's Breath Inn, once a quiet restaurant and bar for some of the local jet set, became inundated with curious visitors to the Peninsula.

Pacific Grove remains the most residential of the upper middle-class Peninsula cities. There are inns and restaurants scattered throughout this small city, but there are no tourist stores. No souvenir or tee shirt shops exist, and no street is lined with restaurants or other amusements. There is no bounded tourist space as exists in Carmel and Monterey. While tourists do spend time in Pacific Grove, aside from the scenic coastline they are not directed to particular activities and places

Fig. 1–2. Symbolic entry gate into Monterey with the emblems of the city's civic organizations on display (photo by Stephanie Alldredge 1988).

designed for them. The city thus retains a feeling of being a "real" place, not one constructed for the outside world.

Monterey, on the other hand, offers tourists three distinct areas to visit: the Path of History, Cannery Row, and Fisherman's Wharf. The city promotes these areas in the literature tourists receive: each area has its own brochure and each is mentioned in general Peninsula brochures. They are also visually framed near and within the city. Signs on the highway and within the city announce these spots as places to visit. Each site has large parking lots, souvenir shops, and pedestrians (a rare sight apart from tourist areas and shopping malls).

The city itself is visually framed by a series of symbols. At the Monterey city line a low wall, suggestive of a fence, faces the highway. It is laden with the emblems of sanctioned civic organizations: the Rotary Club, the Lions Club and other groups. These emblems convey to the visitor the values that the city feels are important to its identity.

Many of the tourist events on the Peninsula are staged events. They have been designed by promoters to draw large temporary crowds to the Peninsula. Examples include the Monterey Jazz Festival, the Carmel Bach Festival, the Hot Air Balloon Festival, and the recently instituted Monterey Film Festival. Each of these events lasts for a concise period (from one weekend to a full week), takes place in a specific location, and is attended by a national audience that travels to the Peninsula for that event. Monterey designed a special area, a bounded space, to house some of these events: the Monterey Fairgrounds. The fairgrounds is a large fenced area of open ground with a number of structures ranging in size from warehouse proportions to small booths. It is located on the edge of the city and is further framed by highway and city signs.

Unlike Carmel and Pacific Grove, Monterey's past includes an important industrial era. Monterey was not created and preserved as a place of natural beauty reserved for leisure. Instead the city's landscape is dotted with the physical remains of its industrial days and a variety of commercial businesses.

Most of the fish canneries were located along Ocean View Avenue, now known as Cannery Row. Empty canneries filled "The Row" for twenty years before developers elected to renovate them into restaurants and shops. Transformed from an area of industrial factories to a leisure environment dedicated to the sale of recreational commodities, the Row today attracts tourists from all parts of the world.

Of all the Peninsula cities, Monterey is the one that most struggles to create an identity for itself. No longer a city of canneries, it has changed itself into a middle-class tourist mecca, a place where people spend their leisure time. It is a collection of written, visual, and verbal texts that, taken together, portrays a culture of advanced consumer capitalism (Dorst 1989:2–3). For whatever reasons tourists come to the area, once they arrive they spend their time in the context of recurrent economic exchanges. Even the Path of History, which counts only two shops among its numerous historic "homes," foregrounds artifacts as examples of a class-based aesthetic. Experience for sale, souvenirs, and specific commodities so define leisure that one tour guide only convinced an older woman to visit the Path of History by describing one of the houses (the Larkin House) as an "ancient Macy's."

The homogenizing effects of a world market imply a certain sense of placelessness. In Monterey, souvenir sea otter salt and pepper shakers that were made in Japan, clothing stores selling dresses from India, and chain restaurants contribute to the idea that the tourist has reached a destination that is not rooted in a particular locale. Although the tourism industry uses historical descriptions in its brochures as a tool to market Monterey as unique, upon arrival it is the commodity from "Somewhere Else" that the tourist encounters. The contradiction in modern mass tourism that Dean MacCannell noted is present in Monterey: the international homogenization of the culture of the tourist and the artificial preservation of local attractions.

Monterey: A Historical Perspective

In the early part of Richard Handler's monograph on *Nationalism and the Politics of Culture in Québec,* he calls into question the "rhetoric of historical narration" that treats the nation as an objective, bounded unit and history as constructed of solid facts.

> Relegated to the background, history can be presented in matter-of-fact fashion as to what is already known or what needs to be known to understand the present-day problems that one wishes to examine....This strategy obliterates any sense of history as story or construct (Handler 1988:19).

The writing of history, just as its presentation in public history texts, involves political choices. The history of Monterey, which is outlined for tourists on a large wayside adjacent to Fisherman's Wharf, has become the official history of the city.

> Monterey Harbor
> Look out upon these waters
> Their recorded history began when Juan Rodriguez
> Cabrillo sighted the "Bay of Pines" on Nov 17, 1542.

> Sebastian Viscaino was first to touch land Dec 16,
> 1602. He claimed it for Spain and named it the harbor
> For the Viceroy of Mexico, the Count of Monterey.

> June 3, 1770 is Monterey's birthday. On that day Gaspar de Portola, the soldier, and Padre Junipero Serra, father of the California Missions, joined from land and sea to establish the first settlement.

> For 76 years this was the capital of Spanish and Mexican California. Here was the Royal Chapel, the Presidio, and the only Custom House. They still stand nearby.

> In 1818 Bouchard, the Argentine Privateer, sailed into the bay and sacked the town. In 1842 Commodore T. AP Catsby Jones, U.S. Navy,

16

under the mistaken belief that war had been declared against Mexico, seized the port but withdrew after three days.

On July 7, 1846, War actually having been declared Commodore John Drake Sloat, commanding a squadron of three ships raised the 28 star flag of the United States over the Custom House, taking possession of a great Western territory now forming all or part of seven states.

Three years later, in 1849, many delegates to the states's constitutional convention arrived by ship.

On these sands in 1879 walked Robert Louis Stevenson dreaming the plot for "Treasure Island."

From 1854 to the early 1900s Monterey was a whaling port and the beaches were white with whale-bone. Sails came to dot the bay. Later in the 1930s here was the greatest sardine fishery in the world.

Look out again upon these waters, Monterey Harbor is small, but it has made history.

In contrast to this sanctioned text, I offer the following thoughts on the kind of history that has been omitted from the official version. This other history concerns Native Americans, Asians, Mexicans, and southern Europeans, and it concerns an industrial economy and the working classes. The thoughts I present below are not meant to be comprehensive, but to note the evidence of that history, however unenshrined, upon the landscape.

Juan Rodriguez Cabrillo was the first European to "discover" the Monterey Bay in 1542, but it was not claimed for Spain until Sebastian Viscaino named it the Port of Monterey in honor of the man who had ordered his expedition in 1602, the Viceroy of New Spain. The Spanish settled the area in 1770 when Don Gaspar de Portola and Father Junipero Serra traveled to its shores from Mexico (then a part of Spain) to establish a mission and a Presidio. Father Serra reportedly said mass for his group under the same oak tree where Viscaino had prayed. When Portola and Serra arrived, they encountered the original inhabitants of the area, a group of Native Americans, the Costanoans, who had been living in the area for some three thousand years. They were soon colonized by Father Serra.[1]

Spain named Monterey the Capital of the Baja (lower) and Alta (upper) California Empire in 1776. The city remained in Spanish hands until Mexico seceded from Spain with the Mexican Republic Proclamation in 1822. This proclamation brought all residents of California, or

"Californios" under the rule of Mexico and marked the beginning of what is today known as the Mexican Period. During the Mexican Period the number of ranches increased dramatically and the trade of cowhides (called California Bank Notes) to English and American vessels became an important commercial activity. Monterey became a port of entry for trading ships, and so in 1827 the Mexicans built the Custom House in Monterey to collect import duties. In 1842 the United States established a consulate in Monterey and appointed a wealthy American merchant living in the city, Thomas Larkin, as the first American consul to Mexico.

In 1846 the land again changed hands, this time to the Americans, when Commodore John Drake Sloat demanded the surrender of Monterey and raised the American flag over its shores. Larkin was certainly instrumental in effecting this takeover. Thus began a short period of American occupation. The Treaty of Guadalupe Hidalgo, signed in 1848, made all of Alta California a part of the United States. Shortly thereafter a constitution for the new territory was written in Colton Hall in Monterey, and California was admitted into the United States (1850). Monterey then lost its importance on three fronts: the designation of capital city was changed from Monterey to San Jose; the port of entry was relocated to San Francisco; and, later, the county seat was moved to Salinas. These events, coupled with the gold rush of 1849 in lands east of Monterey, depleted Monterey's population and the area experienced a dramatic decline in activity. The subdued nature of the early American years has, in retrospect, colored contemporary interpretations of Monterey's Spanish and Mexican periods.

In 1880 the major investors in the Southern Pacific Railroad opened the Del Monte Hotel. This elaborate, expensive resort hotel catered specifically to the rich (its present day counterpart is Pebble Beach). It boasted multiple swimming pools, each a different temperature, croquet courts, archery ranges, a stable, and a seventeen-mile scenic trip along the coastline to a rustic lodge. Today this scenic trip is known as the Seventeen Mile Drive, and a fee is charged to drive its length. The rustic lodge is now called The Lodge at Pebble Beach and is an elite resort next to a world-class golf course. While the Del Monte Hotel suffered several fires in the ensuing decades, each time it was rebuilt in even grander proportions and was known as the "Queen of American Watering Places." One of the only major drawbacks to the hotel was the odor emanating from Cannery Row, where the Chinese community dried fish and fish meal on large outdoor racks. (It is said that three of the adjacent Peninsula cities were known as Carmel by the Sea, Pacific Grove by God—referring to its fundamentalist beginnings—and Monterey by Smell.) The Great Depression forced the hotel to close and in 1947 the Navy purchased the hotel and the surrounding 627 acres for its Naval Post Graduate School.

Although offshore whaling had been an important commercial enterprise in the late nineteenth century, Monterey's fishing industry was really launched in the early twentieth century. The industry concentrated upon catching and canning sardines, with the first cannery opening near present-day Fisherman's Wharf in 1906. Competing cannery owners arrived shortly thereafter and soon Ocean View Avenue was lined with canneries and warehouses. Some fifty-eight years later (1964) the last of the canneries closed when the once plentiful sardine completely disappeared from local waters. The sudden disappearance of the sardine, which had been considered a limitless natural resource, stunned the local industry and brought it to financial ruin.[2] The era of postindustrialism must certainly have been another contributing factor in the fate of the canneries.

The earliest settlers in the area were the Costanoans. They were followed by the Spaniards and later the Spanish-Mexicans and finally by the Mexicans as the area changed political hands. For twenty-two years Monterey was a Mexican territory. During this time several powerful Mexican families presided over the city while the average person lived on ranches or in the city in homes with earthen floors. The whaling industry brought a small community of Portuguese to the area, and Portuguese is still spoken in certain sections of the city. Chinese workers had been recruited to build the first transcontinental railroad and eventually found their way to Monterey in the 1850s. They built their own village along the sea and became fishermen. Victims of a virulent prejudice known as the "yellow fever" that swept through the United States at the turn of the century, the Chinese village experienced a series of fires of suspicious origin. After fire again devastated their village in 1906, the Chinese left Monterey for the last time. Genovese fishermen arrived to set up a fresh catch shipping service to San Francisco via the new railway in 1874. Sicilians were brought to the area to fish for the new canneries in the early 1900s. They revolutionized the local fishing industry with the introduction of the "lampara net" and remained fishermen throughout the life of the canneries and into the present. The Italian section of the city became known as "Spaghetti

Hill." Today Italian-Americans, with a strong sense of their ethnic identity, own and operate most of the restaurants and shops on the tourist Fishermen's Wharf.[3] The twentieth century also saw the arrival of Japanese on the Peninsula, who again turned to fishing. The social and economic life of the Japanese was destroyed by the internment policy of the United States government during World War II and today there is a small Japanese community on the Peninsula.[4] Portuguese, Japanese, Italians, and Mexicans made up the labor force at the canneries. Following the ancient division of labor, men tended to work on the fishing boats while many of the canneries' sardine packers were women.

This, then, is the larger physical and historical context for the specific tourist environments within the city of Monterey.

Notes

1. The present-day controversy over the proposed canonization of Father Serra is a very clear example of the kinds of political considerations that influence historical interpretations, particularly when public history is at stake. The Catholic Church supports canonization, citing Serra's many Christian acts, including the founding of the California missions and a miracle reportedly performed in the 1960s, in support of his sainthood. Local Native Americans argue that, after the Spanish established the California mission system, Native Americans were subjected to brutal treatment that resulted in thousands of deaths and the suppression of a culture that had existed in California for many hundreds of years. They claim that canonizing Father Serra would be a moral and historical mistake, conveying the message that colonization and brutality are good. One Dominican brother agreed with the Native Americans, saying that the present impoverished condition of many Native American peoples is the result of racism signified and symbolized by Father Serra and his missions (*Monterey Peninsula Herald* 9/3/87).
2. When asked where all the sardines had gone, a subject of much discussion, one wry observer noted, "in the cans."
3. Although the Genovese and Sicilian communities in Monterey see themselves as ethnically distinct, the outside world describes them both as Italian. For the sake of clarity, I shall refer to them both as Italian-Americans.

4. In the late 1980s a memorial was dedicated to those Japanese from the Monterey Peninsula who had been interned during World War II. The memorial, a small garden, is located in Salinas.

2

❖ ❖ ❖

The Construction of Public History Texts

❖ ❖ ❖ ❖ ❖

Originally I had used the idea that the writing and exhibition of history is not something preserved from the past but rather "what has been selected, written, pictured, popularized and institutionalized by those whose function it is to do so," as the basis for my analysis of Monterey's public history texts. While I later extended my analysis to other public culture texts, namely tourist sites, I returned again and again to the public history texts, for their articulation of the relationship between past and present acted as a basis for understanding the other sites.

The two major groups in Monterey that are involved in the construction of public historic texts are the Monterey State Historic Park, a division of the State of California Department of Parks and Recreation, and the Monterey History and Art Association, a non-profit public benefit corporation.[1] Together with the City of Monterey Colton Hall Museum, they have concentrated their resources on acquiring, restoring, maintaining, and presenting to the public a series of structures that they call the Path of History. This presentation of the past has become the official history of Monterey and constitutes the public's primary source of information about the city.[2] These public history texts glorify men of European descent and present the American presence in Monterey as an inevitible progression from the simplicity of the Native American to the complexity and sophistication of the Anglo-American.

The progression goes something like this: the mythological period of origins is represented by the Native Americans who lived on the land in a pastoral simplicity for thousands of years, when Portola and Father

Serra arrived and brought European civilization to the area. Portola and Serra are seen as the "founding fathers" of what would later become California. They are credited with introducing Christianity to the Native Americans and establishing a new social and political order. When Mexico seceded from Spain, Monterey entered the Mexican period. This is portrayed as the culture of leisure period in the city's past, the time when fun-loving, musical, colorful people dominated a land full of ranches and when pirates and other adventurous persons controlled the seas. During this period, certain powerful and sophisticated Americans, namely Thomas Larkin, became political and cultural leaders in the community. Due to the cleverness of the Americans, a significant amount of territory, including Monterey, was taken from the Mexicans in a bloodless changing of the flag. Mention is made of the fact that this coup was attempted twice (unsuccessfully by Catsby Jones and successfully by Commodore Sloat) reinforcing the inevitability and rightness of the American presence. The importance of entry into the United States is much heralded by the "living history" presentation of the room in which the state constitution was written. Just at the advent of industrialism, the interpretation of Monterey's past stops.

Ethnic history, particularly that of Mexicans and Mexican-Americans, but as well of Portuguese, Italians, Japanese, African-Americans, and Chinese is almost completely absent from the physical place of Monterey and from the official image of its past. With the exception of a small section of the Cooper-Molera Adobe, none of the historic houses tells the story of an ethnic minority. References to ethnics, when they exist at all, remain at a surface level of presentation, and have often been altered to suit the perceived tastes of the tourist. On occasion, official celebrations are created, which make reference to Mexican traditions (such as La Posada and the Merienda). These are re-created Mexican-like nostalgic events. La Posada [*sic*] is a Christmas procession that comes from Mexican tradition and reenacts Mary and Joseph looking for shelter before Jesus is born. In Mexico it is done on a neighborhood basis and takes place over the course of nine nights. In Monterey it has been transformed into an event that takes place on a community-wide basis over the course of one night and is attended by a majority of Anglo-Americans. Throughout the procession, a mariachi band plays music that, in Mexico, never accompanies the religious Christmas event.

Neither does the city pay heed to the new social history. No mention is made of any social class apart from the middle and upper middle

Fig. 2–1. La Posada in Monterey, Christmas season 1988 (photo by M. Norkunas 1988).

classes. We are left to wonder about the average people in Monterey at various time periods, how they lived, in what kind of work they engaged, what their family structures were like, and how the various ethnic groups related to each other. One tourist guide to the Monterey Peninsula "took a long time and much research" before he decided to say in print that Monterey's Path of History, if intended to bring history to life, was disappointing. While some had even suggested that Monterey's old adobes constituted practically another Williamsburg, this critic contended that few of the houses on the Path of History were interesting. Most of the buildings had been completely altered and the visitor got little idea of what the average person's life was like in Spanish and Mexican Monterey. He concluded with the recommendation that, "what the city badly needs is a middle-class adobe reconstructed as it was, with the outside kitchen, patio, dirt floor, whitewashed walls, and an attached museum with dioramas of a roundup, fiesta, gambling, and other typical activities" (Gordon 1975:4).

What gets produced and endlessly reproduced in the economic, social, touristic, and historic order of Monterey is the image of elite Americans of European descent who control, and have always controlled, the destiny of the city. Complex issues, conflict, and social relations are suppressed in the interest of this generalized image. This message permeates the whole of Monterey's public history and is reproduced in other forms on Cannery Row and on Fisherman's Wharf.[3] Thus public history texts as well as tourist texts are involved in a form of dominance, a hegemonic discourse about the past that legitimates the ideology and power of present groups.

Reconstructed history, such as the Path of History, represents itself as a true, or authentic version of the past. Those who visit the Path of History, be they tourists, locals, or school children, and who do so uncritically, further authenticate this presentation of the past. Thus they participate in a discourse about the past, publicly and symbolically enacted through this series of historic homes, that denies selected ethnic groups and social classes any voice in that discourse. This participation is either willing, or results from a failure to recognize that they have submitted to it.

Reassessing American Historic Preservation

From the 1850s on, most history museums were built by members of the dominant class and thus espoused their interpretations of history. The Mount Vernon Ladies' Association, begun by Ann Pamela Cunningham, the daughter of a wealthy South Carolina planter, created a "shrine" out of Washington's homesite (Wallace 1986:137–139).[4] By the late 1800s, the old patrician elite of the United States had formed ancestral and preservation societies and enthusiastically constructed shrines and memorials, focusing particularly on the houses in which "famous" men had lived. In so doing they associated their class with the "glorious dead" and cultivated a class-based architectural aesthetic. The hope was that such shrines would Americanize the immigrant working class. "The bourgeoisie buckled History around themselves like moral armor" (Wallace 1986:141). Threatened by ethnics and workers, they became convinced of their inherited legitimacy. This was a period that saw the birth of scores of Daughters, Dames, Sons and other commemorative genealogical societies. The past was seen as "better," as a haven for traditional values that might restore the idealized America (Lowenthal 1985:122).

In the 1920s it was the corporate executives' turn to bring their notions of history to the masses. Henry Ford, in Sudbury, Massachusetts, and later in his Greenfield Village, portrayed the "saner and sweeter" life of the past, celebrating the Common Man in a static utopia. He banished mention of war, strikes, and any hints of anticapitalist culture. The benefit of progress was a dominant theme. John D. Rockefeller spent millions of dollars on the construction of a 1790s portrayal of Williamsburg, Virginia, insisting on scrupulous accuracy. The town commemorated the planter elite as ancestors of the Americanism that Rockefeller now represented. No mention was made of the slave economy or of any conflict (Wallace 1985:148).

While the eras of Franklin Roosevelt and World War II took a new approach to public history by emphasizing vernacular architecture and popular approaches to history, the postwar years saw a return to capitalists' presentation of history. Boeing built a Museum of History and Industry in Seattle in 1952, the American Iron and Steel Institute restored seventeenth century ironworks at Saugus, Massachusetts, and the Stevens family sponsored the Merrimack Valley Textile Museum in Andover, Massachusetts (now the American Museum of Textile History). The kind of history these museums initially presented focused on technological developments and ignored the social relations of production as well as class struggles (Wallace 1985:139–150).

In 1935 the Historic Sites Act enabled preservationists at the national level to begin accepting nominations for potential designation as historic places. The National Park Service, overwhelmed with requests, established guidelines according to which a site had to be of "national significance." Regional, minority, or class-related symbols were deemed inappropriate for historic preservation and efforts were directed towards the preservation of prominent structures and patriotic events. Preservationists fell into two fairly distinct groups: those who sought to save a structure because of its historic value or because it once housed an important person, and those who looked mainly at the architectural qualities of a building (Hosmer 1965:261). The criteria for significance made the inclusion of references to social tensions and struggles difficult at best (Bodnar 1986:148).

Ethnic and regional traditions were kept alive by locals and allowed to exist by the state as long as the state could mobilize support for national culture by erecting symbols that reproduced "the structure of domination in society" (Bodnar 1986:149; Lears 1985:570–75). Beginning in the 1960s, activists and minorities began re-examining readings of the past that provided powerful justifications for the status quo. One could now portray the existence of social classes, although still refrain from comment on the relations between them (Wallace 1985:155–57). Still, in the 1960s preservation remained the hobby of a small, well-to-do elite (Lowenthal 1985:387).

Preservation in California: Patrician Societies and Clubs

Preservation efforts in California originally centered around gold rush events. In 1853 the first official state expenditure on historic preservation was five thousand dollars paid to William S. Jewett for a portrait of pioneer John Sutter. In the 1850s several organizations interested in preservation were formed: The Society of California Pioneers and the Historical Society of California. The 1870s saw the creation of several new organizations including the Native Sons of the Golden West. In 1885 the Native Sons began the process of creating the state's first official historic landmark, a granite monument and bronze statue of James Marshall, whose discovery of gold had set off the California gold rush of 1849. The 1880s and 1890s saw mounting interest in California history and historic preservation, with restoration work beginning on the Carmel Mission and Sutter's Fort. The same decades saw the formation of yet more historical associations in California: the Historical Society of Southern California, and the Native Daughters of the Golden West (Engbeck 1980:35–36).

In 1902 the Native Sons of the Golden West organized a group of societies interested in California history into the California Historical Landmark League. Its purpose was to preserve historic landmarks of the state, especially the missions, to place memorial tablets commemorative of historic places and events in appropriate places, to encourage historical research, and to establish a chair of California History at the University of California. It began a major fundraising campaign, enlisting the support of such notables as William Randolph Hearst. As trustee of the cash and real property of the league, Hearst took title to the sites it had acquired and signed them over to the state. Among the acquisition and restoration sites were Colton Hall, the site of the California Constitutional Convention of 1847 in Monterey, the landing place of Junipero Serra in Monterey, and California's First Theater, also in Monterey. Much of the preservation effort took place in Southern California and was directed at the rehabilitation and restoration of the Spanish missions that dated from the latter half of the eighteenth century (Hosmer 1965:125). Like the historic homes in other parts of the United States, the Spanish missions in California represented an era of European colonialism. Native Americans, described as primitive and pagan, were converted to Christianity, taught to dress as Spaniards, and culturally re-educated.

Women's Clubs played an important role in historic preservation in California. The Women's Club of Whittier, the East Whittier Women's Club and the Women's Auxiliary of the Whittier Board of Trade formed the Pio Pico Historical and Museum Society in order to preserve the Pico mansion and to portray for later generations something of the gracious lifestyle of California's pastoral pre-Gold Rush period. By 1940 the Native Daughters of the Golden West had out-organized the Native Sons and were the most broadly based citizens' organization in California dedicated to historical matters (Engbeck 1980:36–39).

The Selective Reconstruction of History

The Monterey History and Art Association (MHAA) is a part of the patrician elite who sees it as their responsibility to save the area's history.[5] The MHAA elected to present the history of the past through a series of buildings that were purchased or left to the MHAA or to the Monterey State Historic Park. According to Captain James Wright, executive director of the Monterey History and Art Association, and deputy director of the Maritime Museum in the late 1980s, the MHAA Board assesses a building's importance and its market price before deciding if the building is worth the effort of fundraising. Going out to raise the money acts as a test of what the community thinks about the historic significance of a building.[6] The stated purpose of the organization is as follows:

> The Monterey History and Art Association was founded in 1931 when it was incorporated under the laws of the State of California. Since the first meeting of a group of prominent citizens of the Monterey Peninsula at

the Old Custom House the [*sic*] latter part of 1930, the Association's primary objective has been the preservation of those reminders of historic Monterey: the old adobe homes and significant buildings of the early Spanish, Mexican and American California. The Association has also obtained through gifts, purchase and loan, numerous articles for exhibition in various historic buildings. It has taken an active part in impressing on the people of Monterey the inestimable value of the City's place in history, the uniqueness of their heritage, and the importance of retaining for succeeding generations of Californians, adopted or native-born, those irreplaceable relics of a bygone age which embody the State's romantic history.

The Association sponsored the Path of History through Monterey which, when followed, guides the visitor to the adobes and historic places in Old Monterey. These sites are also indicated with Historic Markers. A bulletin of historic Monterey, "Noticias del Puerto de Monterey" is issued quarterly. An annual Adobe Tour for the public is held on a date chosen by the Board of Directors, usually the last weekend in April.

Each year in June the members of the Association gather in Memory Garden for a Merienda commemorating Monterey's birthday, June 3, 1770, when Don Gaspar de Portola and Father Junipero Serra landed at Monterey and claimed California for Spain (The Monterey History and Art Association Presents Old Monterey, n.d.).

The Monterey History and Art Association has exerted a profound influence on the writing and preservation of Monterey's history. Several of the town's lay historians are or were active members of the association and wrote the existent local history texts. It is the members who determine which buildings will appear on the Path of History and how they will be interpreted. Through such language as "it has taken an active part in impressing on the people of Monterey the inestimable value of the city's place in history" or "these irreplaceable relics of a bygone age which embody the State's romantic history," the association promotes the idea that its version of history is the only one possible. Ideological control in the present is maintained by control over the past, a control exercised through the "obviousness" of its assumptions. This history then becomes popularly accepted so that those who are controlled by it effectively assent to that control.

Membership in the association is prestigious and confers the right to a possible invitation to attend the annual Merienda, the private celebration of Monterey's "birthday" party when Don Gaspar de Portola and Father Junipero Serra landed at Monterey and claimed California for Spain. This is celebrated each year in Memory Garden, located in the rear of the Pacific House. It is closed to nonmembers and cannot even accomodate all those who pay their annual dues. It is, however, advertised in the tourist literature, as well as being highly publicized locally. The result is a high status party that promotes an association with artifacts and customs that seem Spanish but is effectively closed to Hispanic people (few of whom are members of the association).

The Monterey State Historic Park is part of the state park system in the district of Monterey.[7] The general plan for the Monterey State Historic Park, or the guidelines for the park's development, was written by the Office of Interpretation for the State, located in Sacramento (a three-hour car trip from Monterey). The *Monterey State Historic Park General Plan* (1983) presents the following general statement of its objectives:

> The purpose of Monterey State Historic Park, in the City of Monterey, is to preserve for the enlightenment and enjoyment of the public forever, the remaining features of the second Spanish colony and presidio established in Alta California, as well as structures and other features characteristic of the flow of history and diverse populations associated with the total human experience in and near the City of Monterey. Emphasis will be on the span from the Native American Era through the Spanish, Mexican, and American periods, with special emphasis on the period A.D. 1770–1900 (p. 14).
>
> *Definition of Prime Period.* In accordance with Directive 62 of the California Department of Parks and Recreation's Resource Management Directives, a prime historical period is established for Monterey State Historic Park. This period is 1770 to 1900. Preservation and interpretive efforts will emphasize this period. Such efforts do not have to be restricted to the prime period, but they must be placed in the perspective of events of the prime period (p. 18).

The general plan divides Monterey's history into themes and sub-themes including the Native American Era, the Hispanic Period (Early Hispanic being Spanish and Late Hispanic being Mexican), and the American Period. The plan describes the Late Hispanic or Mexican Period as being well represented at the Monterey State Historic Park. This means that the park, mandated to preserve buildings of historical significance, has preserved a number of physical structures from the

31

Mexican Period. Many of the houses preserved are examples of Monterey Colonial Architecture, a combination of Spanish and New England architectural styles. One half of one of the structures represents a Mexican family. The Native American Era is presented to the public through a section of the exhibit at the Pacific House, while the American Period is represented primarily by an exhibit showing the drafting of the state constitution at Colton Hall.

The Path of History: Creating Social Value

The first president of the Monterey History and Art Association, Colonel Roger Fitch, conceived of the idea for a path of history in the early 1930s to tie together what the organization considered to be all of the historic structures and sites in Old Monterey (Old Monterey being the downtown part of the city and its environs, where many adobe buildings can be found, while New Monterey lies on the other side of the Defense Language Institute and grew up around the canneries on Cannery Row). The Path was, for a time, an automobile path, that one state park guide described as "three and a half miles of windshield history." According to the Monterey History and Art Association's Golden Anniversary Booklet, *Preserving a Heritage*, the Path was designed by Col. Fitch, Mrs. Laura Bride Powers, a Monterey History and Art Association member, and the Monterey Chamber of Commerce. The Chamber of Commerce authorized payment to paint a line on the pavement linking the historic sites. The earliest map showing the Path was published by the Chamber around 1938. Due to road changes and increased traffic, the Path was later changed from a driving to a walking experience. The 2.8 mile route, which winds through downtown Monterey, has been changed only twice since 1938, or so the Monterey History and Art Association claims (*Preserving a Heritage* 1981:11). A state park guide informed me that presently a number of versions of the Path of History exist and that the changes in the map caused some conflict among the association's members and other interested parties. The guide maintained that the acceptance of a map was dependent on membership in the "power structure" that dominates public history in Monterey. There are, in fact, multiple versions of the Path and, depending on the tourist literature one consults, from thirty-seven to fifty-nine sites listed. Many structures are, however, common to all maps.

With the establishment of a pedestrian path, blue dots were placed on the sidewalk in front of each historic building. These are hardly visible and will one day be replaced with blue ceramic tiles.

In addition to the blue dots, many of the sites have been marked with permanent metal markers. This, too, was a project of the Monterey History and Art Association, which designed the markers, selected the sites, and funded the project. Money was contributed by several individuals in the community. The city of Monterey physically installed the markers. The first eleven markers were put up in 1931 and as of 1981 thirty-four markers were in place on the Path of History. These markers, metal plaques on the top of a pole fixed to the edge of the sidewalk, give the name of the building, often its date of construction, and a brief description of its importance. The marker in front of Casa Soberanes, for example, reads:

CASA SOBERANES

Built during late Mexican period by Rafael Estrada, half-brother of Governor Juan Alvarado. Later passed to Soberanes family.

Monterey History and Art Assn.
Courtesy Thomas J. Hudson Memorial Fund.

The blue dots and the metal markers signal to the public that this is a noteworthy site. While the houses themselves are the primary historical texts, the markers are subtexts, a part of the system of inscriptions that institutions of power write about themselves (MacCannell 1979:163). They also serve to identify the institutions of power that inscribed the subtexts. Often these subtexts assume an importance greater than the houses themselves: tourists stop to read them without ever entering the houses to which they refer. The unmarked houses remain undifferentiated, insignificant.

Several different interest groups own the buildings on the Path of History, although the Monterey State Historic Park owns a large number of them. A description of many of these buildings is in the Appendix. Most of the sites on the Path of History are devoted to people of European origin or to Anglo-Americans. The First Brick House was built by Gallant Dickenson, who came overland to California from the East; the Old Whaling Station was built by a Scottish architect; the Mayo Hayes O'Donnell Library was a Protestant church; the Francis Doud House was built by an Irishman; the First Theater by an Englishman; Casa Soberanes, while built by a Mexican man, was restored to its appearance when Mayo Hayes O'Donnell lived there; and Colton Hall commemorates the writing of the constitution that admitted California to the United States. The Maritime Museum surveys artifacts from many regions; the Stevenson House is dedicated to the life of the Scottish writer Robert Louis Stevenson, who spent three months in Monterey; and the Boston Store has been redone to resemble its appearance during the gold rush days. The majority of sites on the Path are houses. Most of these houses were donated to the state by their last owners, or by the descendants of the family who had once lived in the house. The donors represent a class wealthy enough to leave property to the state. Mayo Hayes O'Donnell, for example, was active in the Monterey History and Art Association, wrote articles for the *Monterey Peninsula Herald* on Monterey's history, donated her personal collection of local materials to what became the Mayo Hayes O'Donnell Library (the former chapel owned by the Monterey History and Art Association) and willed her residence, the Casa Soberanes, to the state. The Jack family, a wealthy local family, also donated several of the structures on the Path of History.

The Monterey State Historic Park offers daily guided tours on an hourly basis of many of its buildings. There are thirteen guides who are involved in interpreting the buildings to the public. Other houses, leased to civic clubs in the city, are open to the public on weekends for self-guided tours. The tours guides are employees of the state and receive an informal training. They are apprenticed to the existing guides at the various buildings, and it is from them that they learn about the buildings and local history. No formal interpretive manual exists for most of the buildings, although literature about the history of Monterey is available for the guides to read during quiet working hours. They have a large body of information to cover, as they rotate from building to building and are expected to be able to give a tour of any of them. In one case, at the Larkin House, a permanent guide has been appointed.

The MHAA has never represented itself as being interested in Monterey's industrial period. Apart from the brief mention of the canneries in the Maritime Museum, its interpretive efforts are concentrated on Old Monterey's adobes. A test case arose in late 1987 when the last three examples of cannery worker housing became the focus of public discussion. The houses, one-room structures with a small kitchen, running water, natural gas and electricity, and tar paper roofs, once rented for five to eight dollars a month. By 1987 the land they sat upon, adjacent to Cannery Row and zoned for commercial use, had become very valuable (the asking price for the land was $484,000). An appeal was made to purchase and preserve the houses, but no group stepped forward to assume that responsibility. The Cannery Row Foundation was the organization most likely to fight for the preservation of the houses. Michael Hemp, director of the Cannery Row Foundation, was personally trying to sell a lot next to the shacks for $350,000. He maintained that the shacks were not worth trying to preserve (*Monterey Peninsula Herald* 10/12/87).

Collapsing History into Myth, Leisure, and Linear Progress

My choice of the two houses I will describe was based on what the Monterey State Historic Park considers the most important buildings, and this inference is in turn based on the number of hours the buildings are open, and what the guides told me constitute the priority buildings. They are the Pacific House and the Larkin House. Two other significant structures, the Cooper-Molera Adobe and the Custom House, are described in detail in the Appendix.

Owned by the Monterey State Historic Park and open daily, the Pacific House borders a large open plaza area, known as Custom House Plaza. It is a three-minute walk from the Custom House and a five-minute walk from Fisherman's Wharf. Built for Thomas O. Larkin in 1847, the Pacific House is a two-story adobe that has been used for many purposes, including a ballroom, a courtroom, and a church. Memory Garden, immediately behind the Pacific House and once the scene of bear and bullfights, hosts the annual Merienda. The building was purchased by David Jacks in 1880 and remained in the family until it was deeded to the state by Margaret Jacks in 1954. This information is presented on a plaque in the entryway to the building.

There are eight rooms on the first floor of the Pacific House, each telling something about the history of a particular period in Monterey's past. This is presently the only general history museum in the city, as the Monterey State Historic Park chose this building as the appropriate site to present a "broad interpretive" display in 1968. According to the district historian, this would be the place to tell the story of various ethnic groups in Monterey, were funding available. While the remainder of the Path of History offers individualized buildings with particular stories to tell, the Pacific House is the place where the story was to be synthesized, where there was to be an ideological gathering of the disparate elements. This does indeed occur at the Pacific House, with the museum reinforcing the concept of history found throughout the Path of History.

A complex intellectual and artifactual history has been flattened, and at times suppressed, in the interest of a simplified generalized image. John Dorst refers to Barthes's identification of such images with mythological discourse. These images, myths, are powerful tools of legitimation and hegemony (Dorst 1989:190 [Barthes 1972]). This synopsis of the past into a digestible touristic presentation eliminates any discussion of conflict; it concentrates instead on a sense of resolution. Opposed events and ideologies are collapsed into strong statements about the forward movement and rightness of history.

This version of history locates the beginning of Monterey in the mythological period of the Native American. It is a period in which one senses the unchanging flow of time, a pastoral primitivism. The Native American section physically begins the Pacific House exhibit, just as it serves as an origin myth for the history of Monterey. The exhibit consists mainly of a map of the culture areas of the tribes of California and a number of six-foot drawings and paintings depicting the following themes: a religious ceremony of the Costanoans, hunting and fishing, gathering, a lesson for survival, acorn processing, three Native Americans telling stories around a fire, Native Americans in ceremonial dress, a colored map of Costanoan territory and other Native American territories, and the faces of Costanoan Indians. Finally there is a glass case showing the processes that archaeologists use to reconstruct the story of the past through unearthed fragments. There is an anthropological perspective to the exhibit, the presence of archaeologists, an effort to explain the ways of life of a foreign and primitive people. No other section in this exhibit, or any other exhibit in the city, explains the religion, foodways, and other ethnographic aspects of a people. Suggesting that a people are primitive is a justification for colonizing them. The Pacific House brings us physically through stages of evolution as we move forward through the "primitive" period of the Native Americans, into the more "advanced" period introduced by the Europeans.

The anthropological approach is repeated in the second section devoted to Native Americans in the Pacific House: the Holman Collection on the second floor of the museum. Again, the physical placement of the exhibit is telling. Just to the right of the main door are stairs leading up to the Native American exhibit. Here, the Native American display is set apart from the main body of historical artifacts in a dimly lit, unheated area. The rooms upstairs, in one continuous circular arrangement as opposed to the linear arrangement of the European exhibit, house glass cases of artifacts arranged thematically. The thematic cases cover the following: a map of the United States and South America, baskets and pottery, hunting, gathering, architecture, transportation, war items, religion, pottery, dress, basketry, arts and crafts. Once again, the sociocultural institutions of the culture are fragmented for presentation as specimens of a primitivism. Native Americans are presented as a people in a time of origins with no contemporary existence. They are trapped in this ethnographic present as if they were no longer developing and no longer existed. No sense of conflict inherent in the Spanish colonization is present, nor any description of the Native Americans' later involvement with the Mexican population or their present day interactions with Americans.

Following the Native American room on the first floor is the Spanish story. Once again the story is told mainly through large placards. The first is entitled Bounty and Booty, the second, In the Face of the Almighty, then the Royal Charge, the Adobe Chain, a New Frontier, Bouchard Victorious, a painting of an adobe mission at night, two people in Spanish dress astride horses, and a placard entitled Beyond the Old Horizons. In the center of the room stands a large wooden table with benches, candlesticks, candles, and a small chest. On one wall is a glass case with artifacts from Spanish days: guns, helmets, swords, two figures (Galvez and Vila) and in a second case a *manga* or cape reputed to have belonged to Portola. In front of the cape sits a Spanish cannon.

The Spanish period is described as a time when Monterey was "discovered." The exhibit uses the myth of a new beginning in which a limited group of people, isolated in a virgin natural milieu, is imagined to transform itself into a new social entity, distinctive and bounded. It overlooks what came before by using archetypal symbols like an ocean voyage (Portola's means of transport) or a remarkable land voyage (Serra's walk from Mexico) to sever continuity with the past. The new beginning is used to explain and to justify what followed (Handler 1988:67). The artifacts tell a story of rapid progressive change as the Spanish establish a chain of missions along the California coast, convert the "Indians," and win battles for territory. The vocabulary (New Frontier, Victorious, Beyond the Old Horizons) and artifacts bespeak the advent of a progressive civilization in Monterey, very different from the primitivism of the Native Americans.

The fourth and fifth rooms apparently tell the Mexican period story. They are actually adjoining spaces separated by a kind of entryway. In the first room is a glass case with the dress of a *vaquero* or cowboy, along with cowboy artifacts—a guitar, a chair, and other objects. In the next case are the artifacts of what I assumed to be a Mexican woman—among them a fan, shawl, pottery, and a scarf box. In this room hangs a painting of several women on a balcony in a party atmosphere with men on horses underneath. Below the painting stands a large wooden chest decorated with metal locks. Another glass case holds a Mexican flag, and the final artifact is a decorated chair.

The fifth room shows a glass case with a Mexican flag, candelabras, and books. It is unclear what this is meant to represent. The room houses furniture consisting of a piano, a clock, a mirror, two portraits, and a chair made from an oak tree[8]. Behind a fenced-off area are cowboy artifacts and chairs. There is a marble table outside of the fenced area, with a painting of a man on a horse. Most of the material in the Mexican rooms is not described or labeled. There is no sense of a sequential history of the Mexican presence in Monterey, as one finds in the Spanish room.

Here, as throughout the Path of History, Mexicans are portrayed as fun-loving people. The exhibit highlights their artifacts of leisure—fancy dress, guitars, pianos, pottery. This is the culture of leisure period in Monterey's history, a time unlike the mythological primitivism of the Native American, but far removed from the progressiveness of the Spanish period or the political sophistication of the American period. The portrayal of the Mexicans in the Pacific House and throughout the Path of History falls prey to what David Langum calls the nostalgic view of the Hispanic past. At one time Americans depicted Hispanics as a lazy and indolent people. Later they came to be seen as pastoral, tranquil, and gracious. Neither presents this group in any meaningful historic perspective (Langum 1983:283). By reducing the Hispanic presence in the past to this ineffectual gaiety, they are reduced in the present to insignificant ingredients in the city's political and cultural life. This diminuation of the role of Mexicans in Monterey's history socializes children to believe in the evolutionary superiority of the Anglo-Americans.

The sixth room asks the visitors to imagine themselves on a Yankee trading ship in Monterey. One section of the room, fenced off, is taken up with a fascimile of a ship and some of the goods one might find on it. In glass cases on the remaining walls are ship artifacts, whaling artifacts, women's dresses, trappers' artifacts, and goldminers' articles. In a small central glass case is a model of the ship sailed by Commodore Sloat. This room appears to represent everything else that happened in Monterey or that concerned its residents—trading, whaling, trapping, and mining.

Room seven is a photographic description of People of the Peninsula. No labels explain the rationale for inclusion. No women are portrayed. Large collages of photographic portraits line the walls. Those presented include: Old Gabriel, S. F. B. Morse, David Jacks, Pietro Ferrante, photos of men in working clothes, Armin Hansen, Robert Louis Stevenson, Robinson Jeffers, Jack London, John Steinbeck, Bing Crosby, General Joseph Stilwell, Father Serra, Father Crespi, George Vancouver, Perouse, Galvez, Lasven, Anza, Strong Smith, Vallejo, Pico, Colton, Pizo, Dana, Sutter, Riley, Sloat, Fremont, Sloat's Flagship, Catsby Jones, Sherman, and Stockton. The names indicate that people from outside the Monterey Peninsula were included in the display. Five of the men are authors, two are Catholic clergy, several are military figures, one is an entertainer, and many are political personages. Both European and Mexican men are included. Also in the room is a chest and a glass case housing military items, bottles in a box, and another chest.

Room eight is entitled "Memories of Monterey." Again, it is a collage of photos, this time of various subjects including: sailors, boats, whales, architecture, abalone, squid, and rice, old street scenes, soldiers, harbor views, houses (one of Chinatown), stores, the railroad, hotels, landscapes, bullfighting, parades, and picnics. In the glass case in this room are a watch and various clock-making machines.

It is appropriate that the latter two rooms use collage as their organizing principles, for, after the capture of Monterey by Commodore Sloat and the writing of the state Constitution, the thread of the historical narrative is lost. The city's twentieth century history and people collapse into a series of equivalent images. Bing Crosby (circa 1960) shares a wall with Father Junipero Serra (circa 1770) and Pietro Ferrante (circa 1910), flattened against time.

The exit is the entry, a reception area, where the visitor pays the dollar entry fee, is given a schedule of the tours available in other buildings, and can purchase certain items. The room also contains a glass case with a model of the city of Monterey. In a sales rack near the model are books and posters of California. Along the wall facing the reception desk are a series of placards representing the flags of the countries that were involved in the history of California, most notably Spain, Mexico, Argentina, Russia, and the United States.

The process of decoding the museum is made more difficult by the lack of written information about the artifacts. In some of the rooms there is a sense of thematic organization, and in some a chronological arrangement of the past is presented. After that the displays become more eclectic, showing artifacts and photographs from various time periods and various walks of life. The historical presentation stops at the end of the nineteenth century, in part because after 1900 the city went through a major change to an industrially based economy. In light of the city's efforts to transform itself into a tourist resort area and to return to a nontechnological, nonindustrial image, this recent industrial past is de-emphasized.

Class-Based Aesthetics and Ethnic Exclusion

Owned by the Monterey State Historic Park, the Larkin House is open to the public six days per week. It is the only one of the Monterey State Historic Park's houses to have a permanent—that is nonrotating—guide. According to the head ranger for the Monterey State Historic Park, the Larkin House satisfies the requirement that a building must be of historical significance on two fronts: it was the home of Larkin, the only U.S. consul to Mexico (significant personage), and it is rumored to be the first two-story building in California (architectural significance).

The Larkin House is considered one of the most important structures on the Path of History because of its builder and namesake, Thomas O. Larkin. Larkin arrived in Monterey from Boston in 1835, sent for by his half-brother Captain J. B. R. Cooper (of the Cooper-Molera Adobe, another house on the Path of History), to assist him in his business affairs. Soon after his arrival, Larkin built this house, the first two-story house in Monterey and one of the earliest examples of Monterey Colonial architecture. On the bottom floor of the house, Larkin conducted a merchandise business; the top floor served as his

Fig. 2–2. Larkin House exterior (photo by M. Norkunas 1987).

family's living quarters. From 1843 to 1846 Larkin served as the first and only American consul to Mexico in California. During his time in Monterey (he moved to San Francisco in 1850) the house was a center for social and political activity. It is said that Larkin had much to do with Commodore John Drake Sloat's seizure of Monterey in 1846. The house was out of family hands for seventy-two years when Larkin's granddaughter, Ms. Alice Toulmin, bought it sight unseen in 1922 and moved herself and her husband into the home from Portsmouth, New Hampshire.

In 1957 Ms. Toulmin was the first person to leave a house as a historic monument to the State of California (Hearst was next when he left his castle in San Simeon) and with it all of her furnishings, 150 pages of instructions on how the house was to be presented (including such details as the angle at which a statue should be turned), and a birthday fund. The birthday fund was for a dinner party to be held for the advisory board each year on Ms. Toulmin's birthday. The advisory board, consisting of twenty-four members, flies in for this party, uses the house china, and follows the menu Ms. Toulmin left. The guide explained this on each of the two tours I went on. Like the Merienda, it is an in-group event that receives wide publicity, which in turn increases its prestige.

The guide is a personable woman in her fifties, with long black hair tied in a ribbon at the back of her head. She appears to be from the past herself. At the conclusion of the tour, when the guests were paying their dollar fees and complimenting the guide, she told us that she had "quite a following." She also referred to herself as the curator of the house. Sometime later, when I recounted some of the stories I had heard at the Larkin House, another guide told me that the Larkin House guide, while very popular, sacrificed historical reality for dramatic purposes. My account of the Larkin House comes mainly from the two tours that I took with the Larkin House guide.

The guide explained a bit of the biography of Thomas Larkin and his wife, who were the first American couple in Monterey. The guide spoke of Larkin meeting his wife on board a ship, then wove some of the history of Monterey into her description of Larkin. The majority of the tour, however, had to do with the pieces of furniture in the house, their dates and styles, and their countries of origin. She explained how Ms. Toulmin had moved her entire household of furniture from New Hampshire to Monterey by train, including many of the pieces that had originally come to her from her grandfather Larkin in California. We were told of the family connections, including a gilded egg given by Mrs. Roosevelt, and the horse Larkin's family had lent to Paul Revere, for the "upper crust all knew each other." This information constituted the main points of the two tours I took of the Larkin House.

I later learned some other interesting information from a variety of written sources. Apparently the Monterey Colonial style of architecture became a model adopted by Americans and influential Hispanics seeking to express their prominence with houses similar to the Monterey archetype (Kirker 1986:27–28). It had become important to leading *Californios* (as residents were then called) to live in an American house, and the Monterey Style was transmitted with remarkable speed through the network of Hispanic kinships, centering around General Mariano Guadalupe Vallejo.

Not only was Vallejo the most extensive builder in the Monterey Style but almost every other Monterey Colonial builder was in some way connected with him or his family. Larkin himself was brother-in-law to the general's sister, Encarnación (Señora John Rogers Cooper); another sister, Rosalia (Señora Jacob C. Leese), became the second mistress of the Larkin House when her American-born husband acquired the property in 1849. The much restored Casa Amesti in Monterey was built for a third sister, Prudenciana, and it was she who transformed it into something resembling its present form. Governor Alvarado, who presumably built the second Monterey Style house, was Vallejo's nephew, although they were of the same age. Another well known two-story Monterey adobe, the so-called Casa Soberanes (1841), was constructed for a Vallejo cousin, José Rafael Estrada (Kirker 1986:32–33).

Larkin had been described by a contemporary as a man whom one supposed to be Mexican: dark and thin, dressed as a European except that he wore a serape and a sombrero (Kirker 1986:32). Nowhere on the tours I took did the guide mention any Hispanic influence on Larkin, nor did she describe the influential Vallejo family.

The story of Larkin himself is far more interesting than a tour of the furniture in his house represents. Larkin's first child was the product of his shipboard liaison with Rachel Hobson Holmes, who would become his wife. He had not wanted to come to Monterey, despising the Mexicans, and thinking of the area as the end of the world (Hague 1983:61). Later, having learned to speak Spanish fluently, he became an important go-between in Monterey and represented Mexican-Americans before government tribunals. He was President Polk's secret agent charged with encouraging California's separation from Mexico and later the only American consul to Mexico. "During his lifetime, he was never recognized in his state or in the nation as the most important person in the American conquest of California" (Hague 1983:65).

It was initially unclear to me exactly what the house was meant to represent. My expectation was that, as it was on the Path of History in Monterey, it was a local home, saved to show how an influential local person would have lived. But I was confused on this point by the guide, who continually spoke of the New England furniture, the Chinese armoire, the electic tastes of Ms. Toulmin, and her perfect sense of design. I experienced a sense of temporal dislocation: What time was I in? Was this the story of Thomas Larkin as told through his artifacts or the story of his granddaughter? What was Alice Toulmin's claim to fame?

The house was a paradox of sorts: on the one hand it did not represent the particular past of Thomas Larkin, recovered and presented as a distinct story; on the other hand it did not represent a simple, continuous chain of events telling the history of the inhabitants of the house. It was rather a historical tableau depicting social class and a class-based aesthetic. Through the artifacts of Alice Toulmin, the social standing of Thomas Larkin was described, and, in turn, Ms. Toulmin's inherited class standing. I came to understand that the house is not meant to look as it did when Thomas Larkin lived there, nor to tell the story of his political and social role in Monterey. It is rather a showcase for the furniture collected by his granddaughter on her travels around the world. At one point the guide described the house as more of a memorial to Ms. Toulmin's taste than to anything else. As with other exhibition "period rooms," the museum visitor follows a path that traces the history of design and good taste, displaying only those "things which have class" (see Kulik 1989). The exclusion of any references not only to Larkin's relationship to Mexican culture, but to the powerful Vallejo family, helped to form my conclusion that the history that was presented as past was in fact a replication of the contemporary social separation between the Americans and Hispanics.

Just as the historic homes that were preserved at the turn-of-the-century were meant to Americanize the working classes, so the Path of History is an effort to Anglocize the Hispanic population, and to recreate in a past setting the contemporary socioeconomic structure of the Monterey Peninsula.

The Pacific House and the Larkin House offer two public texts that realize the same official history of Monterey. Each of these instances of interpretation is a sign or, in Jonathan Culler's words, "an instance of the category it exemplifies" (1981:127). They offer social constructions that do not reflect the range of actual experience in the community's past. Both buildings replicate and validate contemporary social structure on the Peninsula. Mexican culture, for example, is not integrated into local culture, just as it is not integrated into the historical exhibits.

If the Pacific House presents an overview of the history of Monterey through 1900, then the Larkin House may be seen as the culmination of that history, although Larkin actually lived in the house in the mid-1800s. The Larkin House is what the city was moving towards, from the moment Father Serra said mass under the oak tree and converted the Native Americans, through the Mexican "culture of leisure," to the artifactual rewards that the American system offered. It is a house whose quintessential message is to establish the inherited legitimacy of a contemporary patrician elite by linking it with the glorious founding father of the American era. It is a site where the value of the commodity form is emphasized, although nothing is overtly for sale. Instead the idea of a cultural and economic aesthetic is foregrounded, in the form of Ms. Toulmin's impeccable taste.

The exhibit at the Pacific House presents a vision of cultural evolution that moves from the simple to the complex. This is the single-stranded history that is realized everywhere in the city's tourist sites. It speaks to the inevitability of a linear history that is progressive, dominant by right of survival of the fittest.

Notes

1. In addition to the two major groups, there are a number of smaller groups, often nonprofit, who are involved in historic preservation and interpretation in the city. While the Monterey Parlor of the Native Daughters of the Golden West never preserved any structures, they were involved in place markers. The Historic Landmarks League was active in Monterey in the early twentieth century. The City of Monterey owns and operates Colton Hall Museum, which includes an interpretive display, a full-time docent, and teacher education programs. The Old Monterey Preservation Society is a nonprofit volunteer association that works with the Monterey State Historic Park. It was incorporated in 1975 and is actively involved in sponsoring special events at the Park, in documenting the restoration of the Cooper-Molera Adobe, participating in living history demonstrations (few in number to date) and working on fundraising. Two of its most important activities are the Cooper Store, where publications and crafts are offered for sale, and Christmas in the Adobes, a special Christmas event that highlights Christmas celebrations from New England (the Larkin House), Scotland (the Stevenson House), a Victorian Christmas (the Cooper-Molera Adobe and the Old Whaling Station), an old-fashioned family Christmas (Casa Serrano), Early California Music (Colton Hall), Mr. and Mrs. Santa Claus (the House of the Four Winds), and a Mexican Christmas (Casa Soberanes and the Custom House). The California Heritage Guides operate out of the Pacific House, one of the Monterey State Historic Park's buildings. They offer visitor

information and, for a fee, tours to groups. The Junior League of Monterey County leases several of the Monterey State Historic Park's buildings. The Junior League, for example, sought the funds to have the Old Whaling Station and First Brick House renovated, while the State did the design work. As part of their agreement with the State, the League opens the buildings to the public one day per week and on special occasions, such as Christmas in the Adobes, or the Annual Adobe Tour. The League's purpose is to train volunteers to serve the needs of the community, either as Board members, or for educational or charitable purposes.

2. Many of the structures and sites that were selected for preservation by the historical organizations in Monterey had fallen into disrepair. The buildings had been valued by the society that had originally constructed them. When that society had ceased to exist, or when the then hegemonic class had fallen from power, many of the buildings slid from valued properties to ruins. Michael Thompson makes the argument that this slide from a transient state where the building's value is on the decrease, to a state of rubbish, where it has no value, is a part of the process an item or idea must undergo before it makes the sudden transition to a durable state. In ·the durable state the item's value increases over time until it assumes an ideally infinite life-span. This increase in economic value is accompanied by an increasing aesthetic value, during which time the structure discards its polluting properties. The institutions of power within a society make the decisions as to whether any given structure will remain in a transient state with no hope of becoming significant, or fall into rubbish and hence become able to leap into prominence (Thompson 1979:7–10, 32).

3. They are manifestations of racism, or the institutionalized and systematic devaluation of one group by another. Non-white and colonized peoples are often presented in *natural* history museums in the United States, thus separating their history from those who exploited and exploit them. Euro-American life is more often depicted within the context of American *national* history (Blakey n.d.:47). This holds true for Monterey also.

4. Eric Cohen referred to a journey to such a shrine of civil religion as a political pilgrimage (1979:191).

5. The present major undertaking of the Monterey History and Art Association is the construction of a new maritime museum. Much of

the association's efforts have been directed toward fundraising for the museum. It houses the collection once at the Allen Knight Maritime Museum and is located adjacent to the Custom House and the Pacific House. The Association is involved in a number of other activities, among them the Annual Adobe Tour. The Tour consists of entertainment and a walk through many of the city's adobe buildings, for a fee. People come from all over northern California for this event. Other activities include an oral history committee, a historic preservation committee, finance committee, costume gallery committee, cookbook editors, the Merienda committee, newsletters, publicity, street signs/path of history, and the museum steering committee.

6. Again, according to Captain Wright, the board members are from various Peninsula cities, Carmel, Pebble Beach, and Pacific Grove, although most of the members are from Monterey. He went on to say that they are the people who usually support the arts and cultural activities, people with generally higher incomes, those involved in business activities. They are usually permanent residents of the Peninsula, people who have been involved in its affairs for a long time.

7. The State of California Park System is composed of five regions, of which Monterey is one. The Monterey Park is one of four entities: Point Lobos State Reserve, a natural preserve, the North Beaches, Asilomar (a conference center on the beach), and the Monterey State Historic Park.

8. One of the most interesting items in the room is the chair with a sign announcing it to be made from the Viscaino-Serra Oak 1602–1770 and presented by H. A. Greene. Although this is not portrayed in the display, State Park guides tell a local legend that the very oak where Viscaino landed, and where Father Serra said mass more than 150 years later, was one day thrown into the ocean by a workman. Someone noticed the act and rescued the tree. The stump of that tree now stands behind the Royal Presidio Chapel in Monterey with a plaque over it—far from the Viscaino-Serra landing site. The remainder of the tree is reputed to have been made into the chair on display.

3

❖ ❖ ❖

The Literary Landscape
and the Industrial Past

❖ ❖ ❖ ❖ ❖

Cannery Row revolves around the interplay between tourist caricature, fiction and history, industrialism and postindustrialism (tourism), ethnic and class representations, nature and the drive to dominate. It is an inconsistent landscape, which alternates between enshrining and devaluing its own rubbish.

The initial issue, which was confronted, appropriated, reworked, and transformed on the Row was the fish canneries. Immediately adjacent to the Pacific Ocean, the street has long been a center for fishing and later for fishing and canning. Lining both sides of the street, the huge rectangular canning factories cut off any view of the ocean or of the city. They represent a fifty-year period in Monterey's history consecrated to industrialism. As in so many other American cities, the canneries, like other industrial enterprises, failed for a variety of complex reasons. In their heyday, an entire social and economic culture existed around them—indeed because of them. They were filled with workers from various ethnic backgrounds who lived in housing near the Row. In the early mornings the fishermen would take their boats into the ocean to catch the sardines that would later be canned. Industrial capitalists owned the canneries themselves.

These canneries came to represent more than Monterey's industrial heritage: they represent a failed industrial heritage. Industrial capitalism represented an effort to colonize in many arenas. The Native Americans in the area were colonized by the Spanish, just as the Mexi-

49

cans were overthrown by the Americans. So, too, did the industrial "fathers" of Monterey attempt to dominate and colonize nature. They invested tremendous financial resources in the canning operations that lined Ocean View Avenue (Cannery Row). Year after year, they fished seemingly limitless quantities of sardines from the Monterey Bay area. Nature had been harnessed to the good of capitalism.

Yet the story did not unfold as it should have. A major problem occurred when the sardines virtually disappeared from the sea, leaving the canning operations in financial disaster. The nation, too, entered a new economic period in its history, as industries searched for cheaper sources of labor. Deindustrialization was not some mystical urge toward a service economy inherent in the industrial order, but a global reorganization of capitalism in which corporations sidestepped organized labor for other parts of the United States and finally other parts of the world. What has emerged is not a deindustrialized society but a global assembly line (Wallace 1987:14). As in other American industrial cities, workers were left unemployed and the huge factory buildings deserted.

In its new identity as a tourist environment, why did Monterey leave the canneries as a testament to this industrial era, indeed this failure of industry, this defiance of domination over nature, when the physical evidence of this past could so easily have been removed? In fact had the canneries been removed, the sea, the victor as it were, would have been revealed.

Instead the past was reinterpreted by the physical transformation of the canneries. The passage of time, historical time and fictional time, initially effected a seemingly haphazard result on Cannery Row. Various development interests, the city's vision of the Row, the California Coastal Commission's rulings on what would and would not be permitted, the nature of the shops that decided to settle, for whatever length of time, on the Row, and the price of land were all factors in the reconstruction of the deindustrialized Cannery Row. The Row appeared to depend more on the winds of fate for a sense of place than on any integrated plan. Although many have burned down, the canneries remain the dominant visual structures on the Row, their large square presence cutting the view of the sea they border. This visual obstruction was itself long debated: whether the Row should be constructed with an open panorama of the ocean, or maintain the striking presence of the buildings that for so long tried to control the sea.

Reinterpreting the past has allowed the city to effectively erase from the record the industrial era and the working class culture it engendered. Commentary on the industrial era remains only in the form of touristic interpretations of the literature of John Steinbeck. Shops and pubs have taken their names from the places and characters in Steinbeck's novels, and markers will one day enshrine both fictional and actual people and places. Tourists are doubly estranged from reality on Cannery Row: Steinbeck's art replaced reality, and tourist developers have in turn replaced Steinbeck's vision with caricatures of the art. A kind of tourist reality results—a streamlined version of the past—in which actual narratives of labor, social class, and ethnicity have been replaced by romance and nostalgia.

The cannery buildings, which have always blocked access to the sea on Cannery Row, continue their visual dominance over nature. They remain barriers to the bay. Their transformation from canneries into empty, abandoned structures and finally into elegant shops, restaurants and the Monterey Bay Aquarium, represents a renewed sense of domination over nature, and over a new economic base. The Monterey Bay Aquarium has again captured nature, much as the fishermen did of yesteryear, but now the fish are displayed rather than canned. The hotels offer nature up as a leisure activity, something to be sold as an experience. Thus, manufacturing has been replaced by a leisure industry (one local woman recalled the days before "fish were replaced by tourists" (*Monterey Peninsula Herald* 10/12/87) and the sense of progress remains. Steinbeck, the only snag in the sanitized progressive presentation, has been recoded to nostalgia.

There is no need to recreate the authentic past on Cannery Row. While the tourist literature makes written reference to the past, in fact the Row is present oriented and makes no distinctions between history, fiction, and reality. The Row is a symbolic construction, weaving together the increasingly vague references to the Steinbeck legacy (a new tourist fiction streamlined and cleansed) the canneries as a physical presence (in their transformed state of "nature displays") into a high status marketplace.

Some Tourist History

Like other parts of the Monterey Peninsula, Cannery Row was originally settled by the Costanoans. With the arrival of the Spanish in 1770, the

Native Americans gradually abandoned their oceanfront fishing. Chinese, brought to California as laborers for the gold mines and later to work on the Transcontinental Railroad, settled on Cannery Row to pursue fishing (Mangelsdorf 1986:2). The growth of the Chinese community in Monterey in the 1800s was paralleled by European immigrants, especially the Italians, who also engaged in fishing as their major commercial activity. Chinese residency on the Row, and their local fishing industry, ended in 1906 when the Chinese village burned to the ground.

Just as the Costanoan fishing stations had been replaced by the Chinese village, so the trio of Frank E. Booth, who built the first cannery in the Monterey area, Knut Hovden, a Norwegian canning specialist and Booth's general manager, and Pietro Ferrante, a Sicilian fisherman who introduced the lampara net into Monterey, built on the ashes of China Point (Mangelsdorf 1986:4). Canneries, packing first salmon and later sardines, lined the shores of Cannery Row and flourished until the disappearance of the sardine in the late 1940s and early 1950s.

"The Cannery Row Shopping and Dining Guide to the World Famous Street" reprinted a synopsis of the Row's history, adapted from Michael Hemp's *Cannery Row, the History of Old Ocean View Avenue.* Hemp described Monterey's canning industry as beginning with F. E. Booth's sardine canning experiment and later inhabiting the coastal road between Monterey and Pacific Grove. The sardine factories dominated Monterey's history and commerce for half a century until the sardines began to disappear in the late 1940s. The last operating cannery, the Hovden Food Products Corporation, was canning squid when it closed in 1973. It later became the site of the Monterey Bay Aquarium. The passage refers to John Steinbeck, and to Ed Ricketts and ends by saying:

> The ecological disaster was, of course, mirrored by pain and human suffering as Monterey's major commercial resource mysteriously disappeared, leaving the once thriving fishing and canning industry to die on its waterfront in a ghostly gray demise.

This passage tells a pointed story. Through innovation and inventiveness, industrial factories were built and flourished, and in fact "dominated Monterey's history and commerce." Fate defeated the success of the commercial enterprise when the sardine disappeared. The major seers, Ricketts and Steinbeck, had forewarned the end, but had gone unheeded. The irony is that the text, ending on a note of the ghostly gray demise of Cannery Row, appears in the Row's Shopping and Dining Guide. The stage is effectively set for a new cycle, an opportunity for renewal. This renewal was to take the form of a chance to reassert dominance over nature.

A Walk Down Cannery Row (1988)

At one end of Cannery Row lies the Coast Guard Pier, where sea lions can be found sunning themselves at certain times of the year. People fish here and the Coast Guard maintains a station. Next on the street is an empty lot, which is being developed by the city as a park. Across from the future park is a large parking lot, once the site of a cannery. It is followed by a former cannery, now housing shops and a parking garage. Also advertised on its doors is the Cannery Row History Center, a project of the Cannery Row Foundation, as yet an unopened storefront.

Two great hotels are then encountered: the Monterey Bay Inn and the Monterey Plaza Hotel. There is a strong sense that you are somewhere beautiful as you walk from the Monterey Plaza Hotel, past the former residence of cannery specialist Knut Hovden and The Chart House restaurant. Suddenly you encounter an abandoned warehouse on the left, and a crumbling stone wall fronting a plot of wild grasses on the right. In a flash you are in the midst of deserted buildings and empty lots. This is closer to the truth of John Steinbeck's novel *Cannery Row* than the elegance of the hotels and inns.

The walk continues past a burlwood furniture store, with massive handmade tables, beds, chairs, and fountains inside. The furniture store is home to the Cannery Row Alumni on Friday afternoons. After the furniture store and a large parking lot (the parking lots always seem large, perhaps because they so often stand on the sites of burnt canneries) is the El Torrito Mexican Restaurant, jutting out over the water. The shops then line both sides of the street.

On the left, the land side of the street, on the site of the old Custom House Packing Company and the Carmel Canning Company warehouse, are the Cannery Row Square Buildings. Inside are gift and clothing shops selling items from around the world. Similar shops continue on the street until a parking lot is reached. On the upper floors of these former warehouses are nightclubs, a factory, offices and more shops. The sea side of the street feels more vacant, although it offers no vista

Fig. 3–1. The inconsistent landscape of Cannery Row: the Monterey Bay Inn, the Monterey Plaza Hotel, a parking lot, and an empty lot (photo by M. Norkunas 1987).

of the coastline. On that side, one finds a hotel and restaurant, and finally another parking lot.

Across the street, in the building which once housed Frank Booth's reduction plant (to convert fish offal into fertilizer), is the Edgewater Packing Company, now a carousel, video game area, and ice cream parlor. Alongside of this are Ed Rickett's Lab and Flora's Saloon, although neither is on the actual site of Rickett's lab or Flora Wood's restaurant.

One hopeful Cannery Row planner had once proposed to develop the portion of the Row north of McClellan, as "Old Cannery Row" (*Monterey Peninsula Herald* 1/3/61). At the intersection of Prescott and Cannery Row is what begins the feeling of a more local Cannery Row. In the buildings of the Old Monterey Canning Company, which opened as a cannery in 1917, sit a collection of shops and restaurants, with a bridge connecting the two buildings on either side of the street. The buildings were rebuilt in the form of the old canneries after a fire

Fig. 3–2. Reconverted cannery: the Monterey Canning Company (photo by M. Norkunas 1987).

destroyed them in 1978 (*Monterey Peninsula Herald* 8/6/78). In the basement on the sea side of the street is the wax museum.

Behind the Old Monterey Canning Company building, again on the sea side of the street, is the Outrigger and beside it sits the Lobster Grotto, two upscale Row restaurants. Next follows an area blocked off because of construction. The Foursome Development Company, the largest landowner on the Row, was finally granted permission to build a hotel on that site, smaller than it had wanted, but centrally located. There then follows pure Steinbeck memorabilia: the actual site of Ed Rickett's lab, as it seems to have really looked and as it is preserved by a men's club, the Wing Chong grocery, The Old Row Cafe, Kalisa's Restaurant, and a few abandoned looking lots (where once rusting boiler pipes had served as houses for Cannery Row residents). The Monterey Bay Aquarium ends the Row.

Somewhere in the middle of Cannery Row, just outside of a parking lot on the sea side of the street, is the bust of John Steinbeck.

In Search of the Literary Landscape

It was John Steinbeck and his novels, particularly his novel *Cannery Row*, which made Monterey's Cannery Row famous. In fact, Ocean View Avenue was renamed Cannery Row in 1958 in honor of the novel, thus marking the beginning of a blurring of reality with a fictional discourse whose importance has come to transcend reality. Steinbeck's bust, the only public referent to the reality of the man, carries the words that open his novel.

For Steinbeck, Cannery Row was both "a poem," and "a stink," "a grating noise," "a nostalgia, and a dream." It was full of "sardine canneries of corrugated iron, honky tonks, restaurants and whore houses, and little crowded groceries." The people who lived on the Row were "whores, pimps, gamblers, and sons of bitches," or, seen another way, "Saints and angels and martyrs and holy men" (Steinbeck 1945:1).

John Steinbeck was born fifteen miles away from Monterey, in Salinas, California on February 27, 1902. He spent his boyhood and young adulthood in and around the Monterey Peninsula. In the 1930s he lived in Pacific Grove, the town adjacent to Monterey, with his first wife. It was during this period that Steinbeck would have come to know the people who became the characters in *Cannery Row* and *Tortilla Flat*: the marine biologist Ed "Doc" Ricketts, the brothel owner Flora and her "ladies," Mac and his boys, alcoholics and street people, the paisanos, and the other down-and-out characters who lived on or near Ocean View Avenue.

Out of this association with the paisanos grew Steinbeck's *Tortilla Flat*, published in 1935. The paisanos were a group of

> olive-skinned men and women [who] were the descendants of the original Spanish settlers who had come to Monterey in 1770. Through years of haphazard intermarriage between the Spanish, Indians, Mexicans, and various other groups, the paisanos had evolved. As a group, they went without formal education and were either unemployable or given the most menial labor to perform (Mangelsdorf 1986:127).

It was not until 1944 that Steinbeck, living in New York after acting as a World War II correspondent, wrote *Cannery Row*. Unlike *The Grapes of Wrath*, *Cannery Row* was a romantic, sometimes whimsical look back at the culture of poverty that he had seen on the Monterey Peninsula and in the Salinas Valley. When the novel was published in 1945, the

Fig. 3–3. John Steinbeck bust on Cannery Row (photo by M. Norkunas 1987).

mile-long stretch that begins Cannery Row at the rocks of the U.S. Coast Guard jetty, and ends at Hovden's Portola Cannery, now the Monterey Bay Aquarium, became one of the most famous streets in the world. The men and women of the 1930s and 1940s that were the subject of Steinbeck's *Cannery Row*, and to a lesser extent *Tortilla Flat*, became the nostalgic focal point for the whole of Monterey's canning history, eclipsing the stories of the actual people who had worked in the canneries.

What can tourists come to know of Steinbeck by a pilgrimage to his Cannery Row? Were they to leave the Monterey Peninsula and drive through the Salinas Valley, they could still see the Hispanic migrant workers bent over their labors in the huge agricultural fields, a scene which Steinbeck compassionately described in *The Grapes of Wrath*. But in Monterey they will not find the cannery workers toiling, or friendly houses of prostitution, or Mac and the boys, or even Ed Ricketts. What they might come to appreciate, were they to indulge themselves in more than a temporary visit to Monterey, is the very radical nature of Steinbeck's perspective. In the highly stratified society of the Monterey Peninsula, Steinbeck's works were dedicated to the poor, the downtrodden, the "untouchables." He was more than empathetic towards those he depicted—he acted as a champion of their cause, much as César Chavez was to do on a political level years later. The tourists who reread their copies of *Cannery Row, Sweet Thursday, The Grapes of Wrath*, and *Tortilla Flat* and who then go on the guided Path of History and down Cannery Row, will be challenged by the kind of history with which they are presented. Steinbeck's work excited the resentment of local people in Monterey, who felt that his account of the community was biased and unfair, ignoring the respectable side of the city in favor of glorifying its bums and prostitutes. Steinbeck was later to comment:

> When I wrote *Tortilla Flat*, for instance, the Monterey Chamber of Commerce issued a statement that it was a damned lie and that no such place or people existed. Later, they began running buses to the place where they thought it might be.

Does a visit to Cannery Row reveal any of this struggle between classes in Monterey? The dilapidated environment that set the scene of *Cannery Row* is rapidly disappearing and the giant canneries are being transformed into stores in which Steinbeck's people could never have afforded to shop.

In 1980 the city described the uniqueness of Cannery Row as its combination of rocky coastline, sandy beaches, old canneries and its economic base as a tourist area (*Monterey Peninsula Herald* 5/27/80). Canneries represented "the values of many Americans in the nineteenth century: the faith in progress, the fascination with technology, the pride in America's growing power and wealth, and the love of grand picturesque scenery" (Sears 1982:2). In addition to the wonders of nature and technology, visitors to other industrial cities came to watch local workers, in what Dean MacCannell would call "work displays." What was backbreaking labor became picturesque for tourists—human labor reduced to caricature. In Monterey there was no need to portray the actual workers, for Steinbeck had created a fiction so real, and so easily caricatured, that he provided a fictionalized work display. The cannery buildings themselves were left to remind the casual visitor of the grandeur of technology.

As in other former industrial cities that were striving to promote cultural tourism, Monterey attempted to create an emotive power of place, a link between the physical place and the mental associations that visitors would bring with them. What were those mental associations? Were they based on the street's famous industrial past? Did the Steinbeck legacy, his transformation of reality into a fiction stronger than the past, predominate? Or, in fact is the high priced shopping mecca and its caricatures of Steinbeck's characters coming to overshadow even the Steinbeck legacy?

What is the relationship between any piece of art and the reality from which it is allegedly derived? Many famous fictionalized landscapes transcend the reality they were once based upon, and in the process art and reality tend to merge in quite literal ways. Literature depicts the physical properties of reality; in turn the reality is gradually transformed to correspond to its image in art. The physical site becomes an attraction because it offers an invitation to participate in the fictionalized image.[1]

People flock to Oxford-Lafayette County, Mississippi, of which William Faulkner had written as Jefferson-Yoknapatawpha County. He closely tied his characters to the people in the area and filled his literature with a sense of the place. Faulkner blended "reality with fabrication," combined the legendary and the actual (Aiken 1977:18).

He had discovered that his "own little postage stamp of native soil was worth writing about," and, "that by sublimating the actual to the apocryphal I would have complete liberty to use whatever talent I might have to its absolute top." By creating a cosmos of his own he was able to act like God, moving people around in space and time (Faulkner in Jean Stein 1958:141).

Approximately 15,000 Faulkner fans from the United States and abroad come to the countryside to try to identify sites and buildings, although as of 1977 no signs advertised the town as Faulkner's birthplace, nor marked the sites he wrote about. Those who go to experience the flavor of the places Faulkner "created" encounter changes that have altered the environment Faulkner knew. Some of these changes are the result of processes any town would undergo; others are a product of the commercialization of Faulkner himself. As Faulkner becomes commercialized, the historical Oxford-Lafayette County and the fictional Jefferson-Yoknapatawpha will gradually blend and become one (Aiken 1977:20).

Fact and fiction have already become completely intertwined in Mark Twain's Hannibal, Missouri (Zinsser 1978:155). Mark Twain, né Samuel Clemens, is an immensely popular writer and, as the site of many of his novels, Hannibal has become one of the best known and most visited literary sites in the country (Curtis 1985:8). Approximately 225,000 tourists from the United States and other countries visited Hannibal in 1982, spending more than $16.5 million there.

Like Faulkner, Twain drew on the town he had lived in for thirteen years to create his characters. Unlike Faulkner's Oxford-Lafayette, Hannibal entrepreneurs have mingled "the real, the imaginery, and the absurd to woo tourist dollars" (Curtis 1985:11). The house that Twain actually lived in is marked by a plaque, but in front of it the white picket fence that the fictional Tom Sawyer induced his friends to paint is also marked by a historic plaque. Across the street is yet another marker indicating the home of the fictional Becky Thatcher, while beside it reality intrudes in the form of a sign showing the law office of Twain's father (Zinsser 1978:158). Stores, restaurants, and shops freely borrow Twain's name to associate themselves with the literary landscape and, hence, reap the economic benefits of tourism.

People are drawn to Hannibal by the creation of a set of characters more real than the author himself (Zinsser 1978:159). They seek to "transcend the medium, to anchor in reality the dreams and characters that are, alas, fictional" (Curtis 1985:14). Some come to seek communion with the author so as to better understand his work. Others come to celebrate the ideal of youth and the age of the American small town, a romanticized past that many feel is now lost (Curtis 1985:12). In response to the search for a nostalgic past, the townspeople talk of accelerating restoration using Disneyland's Main Street as a model. This is yet one step further from a place and the fiction based on that place. Now the fictionalized landscape seeks to imitate a fictive ideal.

While in many cases the copy comes to seem more real than the reality itself (MacCannell 1973:589–99), at the extreme the copy strives to imitate a pseudo-reality.

New literary meccas are being created in other parts of the United States. In 1987 a plaque was placed on a brick wall in Fresno, California. Author William Saroyan was born on Broadway Street, then known as I Street, but as no building exists on that spot, "those intent on preserving his memory [had] to make do with a wall" (*Monterey Peninsula Herald* 11/2/87, p. 34). The article goes on to say that the dedication of the plaque was part of an effort to give Fresnans and tourists a sense of the town and its people, about whom Saroyan had written so lovingly. In addition to the plaque, Fresno named its convention center after him, conducts an annual tour of the places he wrote about, and will erect a seven-foot-tall granite monument near his birthplace. Lowell, Massachusetts, has dedicated a park to the memory of Jack Kerouac. It is a literal literary shrine with great granite slabs rising up in the center of the park, each bearing a quotation from one of Kerouac's works. Tours are offered of the places about which Kerouac wrote and of the houses in which he lived. Tourists make pilgrimages to his grave, leaving an array of mementos on the simple stone.

The tourists who came to Monterey soon after the publication of *Cannery Row* in 1945 were, like Hannibal's tourists, searching for a lost past. It was a kind of time-travel fantasy, less to what actually was than to what was once thought possible (Lowenthal 1985:8). While Twain's county celebrated the ideals of youth and small-town America, Steinbeck wrote of the nobility and innocence of poverty. Those who were "whores, pimps, gamblers, and sons of bitches" when seen another way became "saints and angels and martyrs and holy men." And people had need of another peephole after the devastation of World War II, a need to recapture a fantasized past.

The fictional vision of Monterey's sardine industry, the novel *Cannery Row*, began to appear on bookshelves even as the sardine industry closed its most productive year in history, perhaps a foreshadowing of the dramatic change Cannery Row (the place) was soon to undergo. The decline of the sardine industry made way for the area's literary image to have a greater impact on development.

Years ago, between the demise of the sardines and the rise of the aquarium, Cannery Row reeked of nostalgia. It was a literary watering hole for

Fig. 3–4. Ed Ricketts's laboratory on Cannery Row (photo by M. Norkunas 1987).

anyone interested in John Steinbeck's book *Cannery Row*. Walking down the deserted street shrouded in early morning fog, one could almost see the ghosts of Steinbeck's characters such as Doc and Dora Flood and Mac and the boys. The rusted and rotting hulks of the old canneries still evoked the memory of heartier days when the smell of cooking sardines permeated the air (Mangelsdorf 1986:46).

Some years later this romantic impression was to change. One observer noted that that portion of the Row "not gone up in smoke and flame, has suffered indignities that would have saddened Steinbeck." La Ida's, once a bordello, had become a restaurant, Wing Chong's Emporium was an antique junk shop, the Bear Flag, "that paragon among fancy houses," was an empty lot beside an auto body works, and the Pacific Biological Laboratory was a "private club for mildly roistering and aging professional men" (Crouch 1974:172).

Not surprisingly, the visiting public was often unable to separate the real from the fictional. Dora Flood's Bear Flag Restaurant seemed 'real,' Doc and his Western Biological Laboratory appeared 'real,' when, in fact, the people and the locations were fictions based on the real. Many of Steinbeck's modifications were subtle. The Wing Chong market he renamed Lee Chong's Heavenly Flower Grocery, Flora Wood became Dora Flood, and Ed Ricketts and his Pacific Biological Laboratories was written of as "Doc" and the Western Biological Laboratories. Like Tom Sawyer's picket fence and Becky Thatcher's house, it became easy to mix fact and fiction in the literary landscape of Cannery Row.[2]

The real and the pseudo-real is completely combined in the Spirit of Monterey Wax Museum, housed in the former Monterey Canning Company Building. Through twenty-six scenarios, it represents itself as an authentic reproduction of the people who made Monterey famous. The first scenario is a lifelike figure of Clint Eastwood, a real person, dressed as a cowboy, his fictional film character, while in the background one hears Eastwood's real voice. Later one encounters a large area showing the fictional characters from Steinbeck's *Cannery Row* and hears what I originally mistook to be Steinbeck's voice. After realizing that he was describing the wax characters in the scene, I understood that the voice must be someone imitating Steinbeck.[3]

By 1978 "Doc" Ed Ricketts's laboratory was a private men's club, Lee Chong's an Old General Store and La Ida's Cafe was called Kalisa's International Restaurant. Travel writers wrote of the present day real characters on the Row as being as colorful as Steinbeck's fictional ones. Many businesses had adopted names from Steinbeck's books to sustain the old Row atmosphere, but they were not actual sites. Like the stores in Twain's Hannibal, the entrepreneurs on Cannery Row seek to profit by associating themselves with Steinbeck's name or with those of his characters.

Steinbeck and his fictional characters, rather than the canneries themselves or the actual cannery workers, have become the referents to Cannery Row. With Steinbeck as the focal point of the Row, there is no longer a need to refer to the city's industrial legacy. Rather than anchoring the past in the physical remains of the canneries, it is Steinbeck who is used as the implement of authentication, the anchor to specificity of place, the organizing imagery for tourism on the Row. The humorous, nostalgic side of Steinbeck works very well as a representation of Cannery Row, replacing as it does Steinbeck the social critic, the embarrassing revealer of the harsh realities of the cannery worker and the migrant worker. The past on which Steinbeck based his fiction, the difficult social history of the working classes produced by the canning industry, has been replaced by the nostalgia of the fiction itself. Tourist promoters were faced with the difficult problem of reconciling Steinbeck the internationally known writer with Steinbeck the local who portrayed the worst side of Monterey. To glorify him without recognizing this kind of history required a romanticization of poverty so that the poor became humorous heroes, caricatures of themselves. *Tortilla Flat* and *Cannery Row* provided the material for just such caricatures.

The Transformation from Industrialism to Postindustrialism

What happened to Cannery Row after the sardine source was exhausted? Much of the property passed through the hands of several large development corporations. Cannery Row Properties, after selling all usable equipment from the canneries, leased the space to a number of small businesses, including arts and crafts shops, warehouses and light manufacturing firms. The company planned to demolish many of the canneries and replace them with restaurants, hotels, shops, and recreational facilities (Curtis 1981:45–46). Meanwhile, realizing the tourism potential of the area, a San Francisco financier, Ben Swig, bought up property and pushed for the development of hotels and restaurants. Conflicts with the California Coastal Commission, which sought to protect the scenic beauty of California's coastline through its own vision of development, impeded any construction for many years. The Commission denied a number of development proposals, including those for major hotels, shops, and restaurant expansion. In 1976 Swig sold most of his holdings to the current owners, the Foursome Development Company.

The city produced two master plans provoking controversy between the proponents of development and the proponents of preservation. The 1962 plan called for a move from the industrial nature of the area to lighter commercial and visitor uses. The old Cannery Row atmosphere would be maintained in a section to be called Old Cannery Row, while an area designated as New Cannery Row would be aimed at development in the form of hotels, restaurants and commercial establishments (*Monterey Peninsula Herald* 1/3/61). The 1973 master plan favored development. While it appeased preservationists by including among its goals the preservation of the informality, unique character, and historical atmosphere made famous by John Steinbeck, as well as the best examples of the old buildings, it also recommended allowing the Row to evolve from its former industrial based economy to a new retail commercial, professional, residential, and recreational one (*Monterey Peninsula Herald* 7/19/73).

By the 1980s the map of Cannery Row had begun to show many changes. Old canneries were torn down, renovated, or lost to fire. Between 1980 and 1985 the city of Monterey and the California Coastal Commission approved building permits for a number of projects on Cannery Row, including several hotels and an aquarium.

In the 1980s the Foursome Development Company became a major force in the construction of Cannery Row's emerging image. As an avowedly profit-making enterprise, the company's goal is to see the area reach its maximum tourist and financial potential. The mile stretch of Cannery Row is now geared to pedestrians, drawing people from shop to shop along its length.

Steve Henderson, a spokesperson for the Foursome Development Company, talked about a Times Square ambiance on Cannery Row, a pedestrian oriented aura of excitement, with fine eating places, art shows and galleries, and comfortable hotels. The Row as it stood, he said, is like Disneyland before Walt Disney. As the largest landowner on Cannery Row, the Foursome Development Company believed it had a responsibility to set the pace of development and, most importantly, to determine the kind of development which would take place. In that light they built the Monterey Plaza Hotel as a grand landmark so that projects of less quality would pale by comparison. An aggressive approach to shopping had to be taken to bring up the value of the Row so that the area would become a shopping mecca with high quality items. Upper middle-class visitors would be the primary tourists on the Row, although the Monterey Bay Aquarium, another quality enterprise, would continue to draw families.

As for the references to Steinbeck, Henderson wondered how long people would continue to be attracted to Cannery Row based on its literary associations. In the future, Steinbeck, in terms of Cannery Row, would become less and less significant. What would later be identifiable on Cannery Row would be its aquarium, its hotels, and its exclusive shops. The wax museum on the Row was a part of the revitalization and would one day feature a movie on the history of the Monterey experience, promoting its lore and legend. While the hope is to upgrade the quality of goods sold on the Row, there will always be a need for banners and Tee shirts. The point is to get people to come there to shop (interview with Steve Henderson 11/10/87).

Michael Hemp, Executive Director of the Cannery Row Foundation, offered another vision of Cannery Row. According to Hemp, life on the Row was Steinbeck oriented before the aquarium came in 1984, with vacant canneries and people coming to chase the Steinbeck dream, although nothing was done on an official level to preserve that atmosphere. "Steinbeck's historic Cannery Row as a phrase was the umbrella under which nothing was really pursued to establish either its history or Steinbeck—it was just good enough to use that as a phrase" (interview with Michael Hemp 10/21/87).

On February 17, 1983, Hemp founded and directed the Cannery Row Foundation, the only organization in Monterey that concerned itself with the history of Cannery Row. One of the major undertakings of the Foundation has been to hold an annual Cannery Row Reunion of former cannery workers and fishermen. Hemp stated that he hosted the reunions in part to identify people to be tape-recorded and said that he had recorded over four hundred interviews. The "Cannery Row Alumni," as Hemp calls them, are the actual people on whom Steinbeck based his fiction. They not only gather for annual reunions, but they are written up in newspapers and travel books. They meet daily at 9 a.m. in The Old Row Cafe where Charlie Nonella (a former alcoholic and one of Steinbeck's character models) and Hemp are regulars. The old timers also have a Friday afternoon get-together at the burlwood furniture store on Cannery Row. They are a club of sorts, a part of the underground life on Cannery Row. Just as the Row sports contradictions in its physical structure, deserted lots beside elegant restaurants, so too does it contain contradictions in its social structure: the Alumni represent a working class or street society that coexists with the emerging elite image of the Row. Like many of the canneries, the street people Steinbeck made famous, once considered "human rubbish" who embarrassed the city, have also been cleaned up. They may remain street people only in the wax museum, where they are parodies of their real selves. The present reality of Cannery Row uses elegant reminders of the "rubbish" that made it famous, be it beautifully renovated canneries or street people organized into a group distinguished as Alumni, although the city is becoming increasingly impatient with the existence of actual rubbish, deserted buildings, or real street people.[4]

Another project of the Cannery Row Foundation was the 1986 publication of *Cannery Row, the History of Old Ocean View Avenue* by Michael Hemp. The dedication is to "the Cannery Row Alumni—The Men And Women Who Worked Its Canneries And The Men Who Braved The Pacific For Its Silver Harvest." In the book Hemp creates a map of Cannery Row, indicating the location of all former canneries, historical landmarks, and points of interest in Steinbeck's fiction. Based on these historical and literary locations, in the 1980s the city of Monterey designated twenty sites to receive bollard markers indicating the name of the site "at its historic or Steinbeck-literature period" (Memo from the City of Monterey 3/25/87 re: Cannery Row "Points of Interest" Marker Program-Bollard Cap Design). The bollards would only be placed on those sites for which markers had been requested (and funded) by adjacent property owners.

Other efforts of the Foundation met with less success. The Cannery Row Workers' Memorial Park was conceived by Hemp and approved by the city. The park would have housed artifacts mentioned in Steinbeck's *Cannery Row*, such as the large pipes and boilers that served as housing for his characters. Literal rubbish, rusty pipes and discarded boilers, was to acquire social value, as it became a referent to Steinbeck, enshrined in a public park. Plans for the park's construction were halted, however, when the Courts ruled that an adjacent property owner legally owned half of the park's land (*Monterey Peninsula Herald* 10/25/86). The Foundation was also interested in purchasing the (actual) purse seiner that Steinbeck and Ricketts took to Baja in 1940 (featured in Rickett's journal, which Steinbeck transformed into *The Sea of Cortez*). Finally, the Foundation attempted to begin a museum to support the Steinbeck legacy and to tell the story of the canneries and the disappearance of the sardines. As of 1988 the museum did not exist.

After the canneries left Cannery Row, it "existed for a long, long time as a kind of ghost town," according to Hemp. The Row's story, its industrial theme, is a common one in America, according to Hemp, and, without Steinbeck, would probably have had as much historical significance as Sutter's Mill. People came to Cannery Row in anticipation of going back to a simpler time; they came with a sense of nostalgia, searching for an era when poverty had had an idyllic freedom about it. This is the sense of the past that Steinbeck's fiction created for the area. It was only the romantics, Hemp said, who could visualize the past, who were moved by what was left, for there was neither a literal portrayal of history on the Row, nor a nostalgic recreation such as the Cannery Row Workers' Memorial Park. After the canneries began burning down in the 1970s, the street was left with concrete foundations, empty lots, and big industrial-style buildings full of shops. Today, Hemp said, that is it, that is what the tourist sees.

Tourism and the Postindustrial Landscape

At either end of the Row lies its two most imposing canneries. That part of Cannery Row bordering Pacific Grove is the home of the Monterey Bay Aquarium. Built on the site of the former Hovden Cannery, the last operating cannery on the Row, the aquarium opened its doors to the public in 1984. The aquarium was a large draw for tourists, much more so than even the most optimistic forecaster had imagined. Initially it engendered bitter resentment from Row merchants, as it competed with them in the sale of souvenirs while enjoying tax exempt status and took up much of the available parking. Since that time the feud has quieted, with both sides compromising.

The aquarium had become more than just a tremendous tourist attraction. It represented a scientific achievement, which both the fictional and the factual Ed Ricketts would have dreamed about: preserving and studying local marine life. Without allusion to the literary landscape, the aquarium became a commercial success and a center of cultural activity in the city, hosting charity affairs, receptions, concerts, and other cultural events.

The aquarium served yet another, unspoken, goal. It acted to reinterpret the past, to reassert control over a nature that disallowed colonialization. The aquarium recaptured nature and reasserted its dominance by enclosing nature in a confined space, offering it up for display much as the Native American artifacts are offered up for display in the Pacific House in Monterey. Hence, the lesson is that the sea, nature, did not control man, did not win over capitalism, but was in the end subdued.

Near the other end of the mile-long Cannery Row sits another multimillion dollar edifice, the Monterey Plaza Hotel. Just before it, one encounters a smaller hotel, the Monterey Bay Inn. Its promotional literature claims that Cannery Row stands as "a monument to decades of dependency on the Pacific waters for the community's livelihood." It goes on to say that Monterey's newest architectural symbol is the Monterey Bay Aquarium, but "For those who look to experience the rich marine life beyond the confines of this fascinating yet clinical manmade environment, the nearby Monterey Bay Inn offers the facilities for explorers to mingle with sea life in the coastal waters of Monterey Bay." It promotes itself as the inn for divers and others interested in nature. Here the tourist literature on the Row offers a metacommentary, as one site describes and critiques another, defining the aquarium as a "clinical manmade environment," which offers up nature as a cultural display. The Monterey Bay Inn also commodifies nature, but in a less controlled environment.

The Monterey Plaza Hotel acts as the second symbolic gate to Cannery Row. According to the hotel's own promotional literature, the 290-

Fig. 3–5. The Monterey Bay Aquarium (photo by M. Norkunas 1987).

room oceanfront, grand luxe resort signals a "return to the enchant-
ment at this seaside community, which once attracted the world's rich
and famous to the shores of this resplendent resort destination." Its
architecture is meant to reflect a sensitivity toward historical, aesthetic,
and cultural concerns by incorporating the design influences of California Spanish and Far-Eastern elements dating back to the seventeenth
century, the Grand Mansion Era circa 1899 to 1940, and Monterey's
colorful Cannery Row Period circa 1945. The Grand Mansion influence
is reminiscent of the Del Monte Hotel and the Murray Mansion, which
once stood near to where the Monterey Bay Hotel stands today. The
hotel's designers paid particular attention to continuing the flavor of
the Row. They created two second-story bridges reflective of the Cannery Row period (once used to transfer sardines from the seaside factory to the landside warehouse) and "created the spatial experience that
canneries offered" through the placement of the hotel's three buildings
standing "hard against the street." Just as the canneries cut off most of
the bay view along Cannery Row, so too do the hotels.

Fig. 3–6. The Monterey Plaza Hotel (photo by M. Norkunas 1987).

Like the aquarium, the Monterey Plaza Hotel represents a control of the industrial past, a reinterpretation and re-presentation that reveals the success of capitalism and reinforces the class structure. The working-class inhabitants of the Row have been replaced by the hotel's upper-class patrons; the hotel's relationship to nature, like that of the canneries before it, is one of dominance. Rather than capturing and canning fish, the hotel promotes them as part of a leisure activity.

It is fitting that these two institutions, the Monterey Bay Aquarium and the Monterey Plaza Hotel, mark the entryways to the new Cannery Row, for they represent the character that developers hope the Row will assume. At one level they are very much alike: the Monterey Plaza Hotel caters to the wealthy and, as one gallery owner told me, while it is as yet too grand for the present state of Cannery Row, it sets a tone of elegance for future enterprises to emulate. The aquarium, at the other end of the Row, hosts its own galas and receptions. The aquarium and the hotel stand in contrast to the ambiance of innocent poverty that Steinbeck captured in his literature, and which some tourists still nostalgically seek out.

Like the pilgrims to William Faulkner's landscape, those who now come to the Row in search of Steinbeck's fictionalized vision of life as portrayed by his characters in the novel *Cannery Row* will be disappointed. Time has altered both Steinbeck's "history that never happened," as well as the reality of Steinbeck's Row, removing the lower classes, the very lifeblood of Steinbeck's story. Instead they will see copies of what was once real or even complete fabrications that base their appeal on references to Steinbeck.

Developers on Cannery Row are disinterested in focusing tourist attention on what was once considered "rubbish." Street people, factory workers, and abandoned boilers and rusty pipes have been banished. They represent a class of local society and a mixture of ethnic groups from which the community would like to disassociate itself. The movement today is toward recreating the elegant era of the Del Monte Hotel through such structures as the Monterey Plaza Hotel and the Monterey Bay Aquarium. And yet the street gained international recognition only when Steinbeck glorified its human "rubbish" in his literature; the Cannery Row Foundation would like to enshrine the rusty pipes and other rubbish from the past in a public park; and many travel writers see the emotive power of Cannery Row as stemming from the remains of the "rotting hulks of the old canneries."

As on the Path of History, the system of markers and sites is complex and conveys multiple messages. The actual street was renamed for its marker (the novel *Cannery Row*), while the marker fictionalized the real street. Reality was altered to resemble fiction so that it could better represent the fiction's reality. Steinbeck's statue certifies that this is the authentic Cannery Row, but it has gone beyond being a marker of the street and the novel based on the street and has become a site in and of itself. Ed Ricketts's Lab is a saloon across from the site of the actual Ed Ricketts Lab, which is now a private men's club. No prostitutes or "street people" are to be found living on the street—characters from Steinbeck's fiction whose reality would disturb and perhaps frighten tourists.

Notes

1. Some literary shrines have resisted the impulse to remake reality in the image of art, perhaps because the reality is deeply based in nature.

Travellers to Walden Pond come in search of the inspiration that an environment provided to an American thinker. Sitting on the banks of the clear and quiet pond, which Henry David Thoreau described in such detail, they try to understand the passage of life as Thoreau saw it mirrored there. Little remains of Thoreau's presence, apart from a marker on the site where his cabin once stood, and yet people come there to know and understand him better. Apart from some recreational changes, such as the construction of a beach house and sandy beaches, developers have done little to alter the environment.

2. At Bullwacker's Restaurant and Pub on Cannery Row in Monterey, the back of the menu offers an explanation entitled "Where am I?" It accurately describes the building as having once been the site of Flora Woods' bordello, made famous in John Steinbeck's novel *Cannery Row*. It goes on, however, to tell the story of Captain Bullwacker, who came to Monterey in search of the then-depleted sardines and, humiliated, had twice gone around the world in his efforts to bring the sardines back to Monterey. It ends,

> Although Bullwacker hasn't returned yet, locals do remember that the Captain enjoyed a good, affordable, friendly restaurant. Bullwacker's Pub and Restaurant continues in this tradition, honoring the old Captain by offering modern day folks good food and drink in comfortable surroundings.

When I questioned one waitress who works in Bullwacker's, she told me the story of the Captain was completely falsified, or in her words "all made up."

3. Just on the outside of each scene is a small placard describing the person or event represented. While what is written tells some part of actual history, it is a collapsed and altered story. Most of the Mexican women, for example, are portrayed as beautiful and as the romantic liaisons of a well-known Monterey male. The other figures represent the Spanish "founders" of Monterey, two Mexican bandits, three American explorers and fur traders, three writers, one important Mexican political figure (Alvarado), Thomas Larkin, a goldminer, a blacksmith, and a group of "Indians" building the missions, as well as the scenes from Steinbeck's novel. The public accepts these shortened "histories" as literal facts: while I was visiting the museum I overheard several people commenting on the history they had learned there.

4. Once in Michael Thompson's transient category (Thompson 1979), the canneries slid into rubbish. They deteriorated to the point where it became more profitable to sell the old canning machines inside than to sell entire structures, or to burn the buildings down for insurance money. Even in their heyday the canneries were involved in converting rubbish to a usable item: fish offal was ground into fertilizer, a more profitable enterprise, according to Michael Hemp, than actually canning edible fish. From its earliest days, when the Chinese dried fish on outdoor racks, to the later grinding of the offal, the odor from the canneries was as offensive as any rubbish. Even today, many of the buildings on the Row appear to be in the rubbish category. Ed Ricketts's lab is a forlorn looking building, as are some of the other structures lining the street. Michael Hemp had actively solicited the preservation of actual items of rubbish when he attempted to install in an outdoor park the boilers and pipes that Steinbeck's characters had used as living quarters. The pipes were not installed, and I question whether Ricketts's lab will remain in its present condition if the men's club ever decides to sell it. As Thompson points out, rubbish is socially defined, and the boundary between rubbish and nonrubbish moves in response to social pressures (1979:11).

4

❖   ❖   ❖

Nature, History, and Ethnicity

❖   ❖   ❖   ❖   ❖

The series of relationships evident in the texts found on the Path of History and on Cannery Row are also present on a small pier filled with shops and restaurants known as Fisherman's Wharf. The Wharf, once an active fishing wharf, had fallen into disrepair (rubbish) and was eventually saved and transformed into a tourist area. Adjacent to it is a new fishing wharf, but tourists come to see the reproduction rather than the real wharf. Just as in the other two sites, Fisherman's Wharf highlights the city's denial of its ethnic past. On the Wharf, this can be read in physical details: ethnic societies have been allowed to create ethnic monuments and statues but they have been relegated to marginal areas, just off the tourist paths. While promoters cite historical references to attract tourists to the Wharf, little remains on the Wharf to remind tourists of what it once was. And as on Cannery Row, the Wharf has developed a particular relationship with nature.

In a sense, nature on Fisherman's Wharf has been "tamed," Disneyfied to the point that it can be sold as an experience to tourists; so too have history and ethnicity been tamed. Nature is represented as having been colonized by man, wildness domesticated. It appears closer to an ideal of what nature should be rather than what it is. The sea lions, otters, and pelicans all have a staged quality, as though they are performers in the Wharf's theater, entertainment for the tourists. The souvenir shops and restaurants have also colonized nature. By commodifying nature, either in the form of a souvenir shop's bird sculpture or a restaurant's bouillabaisse, the wildlife has been transformed into an image of itself. To hold a wooden salmon in the form of a sculptural representation, or to eat it is a way of subduing and controlling nature. In a sense there is no untamed nature on Fisherman's Wharf, just as there are no unmarginalized ethnics: both are subjects whose essences have been removed in the interests of the touristic experience.

Enshrining a Tourist Space

The process of "sight sacralization" (MacCannell 1976:43–45) begins long before one arrives at the actual site of Fisherman's Wharf. Tourist literature describing both the historical importance and contemporary attraction of Fisherman's Wharf acts as a marker, identifying the site as worthy of being seen. Throughout Monterey and on the major highways leading to the Peninsula, the signs indicating the direction to Fisherman's Wharf act as secondary markers; framing, or establishing an official boundary around the site, further enhances its importance. The large parking lot located between Fisherman's Wharf (Wharf No.1) and the commercial fishing wharf (Wharf No.2) acts as a boundary and site marker on one side of the wharf, indicating to tourists that something important is present—something that many people have come to see. From the metered parking lot it is a five-minute walk to the touristic Fisherman's Wharf. The parking lot and the walkway to the wharf have themselves been marked with plaques: one tells the publicly sanctioned history of the Monterey Bay, another commemorates an Italian mayor, and a third briefly describes Commodore Sloat's capture of Monterey. The very bay, filled with boats (artifacts of leisure) and birds (tamed nature) and the horizon (wild nature), acts as both part of the attraction of Fisherman's Wharf and as a subtext, a metaphor for the kinds of relationships inherent in the presentation created by the Wharf. All of this, the wharf, the walkway, and the bay, has been reproduced in photographs, models, and prints, so that when tourists arrive at the actual sites they understand that they are at "The Real Thing," an authentic site worthy of having been reproduced.

On the land side of the walkway to Fisherman's Wharf lie the Southern Pacific Railroad tracks, now abandoned. Ten yards beyond the tracks is the Custom House. It is a reminder, should the visitor seek out the information, of the days when cargo was brought from trading ships into the building for inspection. Tourists understand that the Custom

House is not a part of Fisherman's Wharf, not a part of the site they have come to see. While the Path of History and Fisherman's Wharf are thematically linked by their common history, experientially and spatially they are very different and their markers, their framing, clearly indicate this. Many more tourists visit Fisherman's Wharf than the Path of History, for the Wharf's touristic space is more clearly bounded. Commodities, a critical ingredient in touristic space, are omnipresent, and the experience itself is modeled after idealized visions of nature.

The Wharf's annual calendar is divided into cycles, some of which are heavily tourist oriented. Winter and early spring are the whale-watching season, when the migrating whales can be seen from chartered boats. The summer months are devoted to the tourists who flock to Monterey and Fisherman's Wharf. After Labor Day the tourist activity quiets down, although it never completely stops, until it reaches its low in December. This seasonal tourist variation holds true for much of the Peninsula, although efforts are being made to schedule events to attract touists in the off-season.

Converting the Real into the Pseudo-real

Each of the three tourist districts in Monterey was once something else: the houses on the Path of History were actual dwellings inhabited by generations of people, the cannery buildings on Cannery Row were functioning factories, and Fisherman's Wharf was an operating fishing wharf. Over time each of the three sites assumed a new identity so that the houses on the Path of History became museums, and the factories on Cannery Row and the old fishing wharf became shops and restaurants. While there was no need to inhabit the museums on the Path of History, nor to can sardines in the factories, an active fishing industry dictated a real need for a functional fishing wharf. By the 1930s the original wharf could not withstand yet another repair. Threatened with destruction after its ability to serve the needs of fishermen ceased, a citizens' groups circulated a "save the Wharf" petition. The old wharf was "saved" and a new commercial wharf was constructed immediately adjacent to it. These dual realities continue to mirror each other. An authentic commercial fishing wharf, not a tourist attraction, and a reconstructed nonfishing wharf, very much a tourist attraction, stand side-by-side in the Monterey Bay. The pseudo reality has assumed prominence over the reality.

Thomas Oliver Larkin built the first wharf at the Custom House site in 1845, just one year before the American occupation of the city. The wharf cost $8,000, and was constructed of stone quarried by captured military deserters, Native Americans, and civil prisoners. Estaban de la Torre provided the stone at one dollar a cartload, and Larkin purchased the wood piles for four dollars each from an English settler. Today a group of stones remains to indicate the original location of this wharf (between the first two buildings on the right as one enters Fisherman's Wharf). At this time the Portuguese came to the area to do offshore whaling, living in the Whaling Station adjacent to the old wharf. The Old Steel Wharf, or the Narrow Gauge Wharf was located a short distance away, near the Old Pacific Depot. It collapsed one Sunday in the early 1800s. An old Booth Wharf jutted out into the bay from the original Booth Cannery to the west of Fisherman's Wharf, part of which can still be seen on the drive from Monterey to Pacific Grove. The Oil Pier was located north of the present breakwater and the Coast Guard Pier. It was destroyed by fire in 1924 (*Monterey Peninsula Locale* Fall 1965:5). By 1923 the Wharf had been repaired a number of times when part of it collapsed, dropping 20,000 cases of sardines into the Bay (*Monterey Peninsula Herald*, n.d.). At this point the city considered demolishing the wharf. Finally the city built a commercial wharf for the fishermen, and the old wharf was turned over to restaurants, jewelry shops, art galleries, boat concessions, fishing excursion boats, pleasure cruises, and other gift shops consecrated to tourism.

Some fishermen remember Monterey as a ghost town before the fishermen came. Later, they told of fishermen earning $1,000 in twenty days and spending their entire earnings in one night at the Bear Flag Restaurant and brothel on Cannery Row. In the 1960s they thought of themselves as the "Last of the Mohicans" (*Monterey Peninsula Herald* 5/5/62). Jack Balbo, an old-timer on Fisherman's Wharf, remembered when, in 1915, his uncle built a wholesale fish market on the Wharf. In 1985 it was a restaurant. Prior to World War II the Japanese worked the Wharf, and women sat outside the fish shops, pounding abalone steaks until they were tender. At that time the Wharf had only three restaurants interspersed between its many fresh fish markets. As early as 1919, businesses other than fishing interests competed for space on the Wharf, but the fishermen and maritime shops felt that fishing concerns should come first. Gradually, the shops began to assume priority, and when fishermen came to mend their nylon purse seine nets on Fisherman's Wharf, tourists gathered to watch. It was at this point—when the work of the Wharf had been transformed (however inadverently at first) into a work display performed for tourists—that the Wharf fully realized its new identity. By World War II the wharf had become a tourist attraction.

On the Tourist Wharf

The entry to Fisherman's Wharf is foreshadowed by a series of markers. Several entry markers in particular signal the visitor as to the kind of experience he or she may expect on the Wharf. From a distance one can see tables on the patio of a small cafe and beside it are dessert shops with signs announcing "Pastries" and "Ice Cream." Coming closer, one notices the art and souvenir shops on either side of the road, large glass windows revealing their wares. Just before the shops is a prominent sign proclaiming this as Old Fisherman's Wharf. The sign is made of wood and appears weather-beaten. It tells a short story: that the Wharf was built of stone in 1846 and gave way to a commercial wharf when the fishing industry became important in Monterey. It concludes, "Despite many changes the wharf today retains the tone and flavor of the past—a monument to the fishing industry and the fishermen who braved the wind and sea." The sign is not alone, for just in front if it is a large metal anchor. These entry markers, together with the birds perched on all the rooftops and the sounds of the sea lions would tell the alert visitor everything. The sign is made to look as one imagines the wood of a well-used dory might appear: worn by the wind and the rain; the anchor, once a work tool, now marks an atmosphere of leisure. Whatever the Wharf once was, today it is a place for tourists to eat and drink, to go on fishing and whale watching trips, to feed the sea lions and birds, and to shop for souvenirs and art.

Visitors told me that they had expected the Wharf to be larger, perhaps comparing it to the wharf and piers in San Francisco. It is difficult to judge its size from the promotional literature. Had the visitor stopped by or called the Monterey Peninsula Chamber of Commerce, he or she might have received a brochure about Fisherman's Wharf telling a detailed version of its past. It concludes, "So, look out upon these waters and feel our adventurous past before you. Monterey Harbor is small, but its history is unparallelled." Nothing but the imagina-

Fig. 4–1. Old Fisherman's Wharf sign and anchor, the left entry marker to Fisherman's Wharf (photo by M. Norkunas 1987).

tion links the past with the present on the Wharf. Instead, the Wharf itself is a literal taxonomy of texts and subtexts about the present, the most important of which concern human's relationship with nature in the context of tourism.

The Wharf juts out over the ocean with two finger wharves stemming from the main structure. All around are boats and sea animals and birds. Here people are walking (vehicles, aside from delivery trucks, are not permitted on the Wharf), strolling one might say. The space they move through is linear, open in the middle and lined with buildings offering objects and foods designed to please. There are no public benches on the Wharf. The absence of benches, in this pedestrian environment, encourages people to rest in the context of a consumer transaction—buying a meal or a drink in a restaurant.

The buildings face right into the Wharf and are of varying shapes, sizes, and colors. In fact when a limitation of maximum buildout was proposed for the Wharf, one city councillor worried that its effect would be to encourage all buildings to expand to the limit. The ragged outline the buildings form, so "vital to the atmosphere of the wharf," would disappear (*Monterey Peninsula Herald* 1/3/62). This does not seem to have happened.

Unique to the Wharf are the city-approved sidewalk signs. They are large placards, announcing the fare of the shops, placed along the sides of the pedestrian area. Food and beverages are also sold on the sidewalk. The food is outside, on large covered counters, to be eaten or drunk (except for beer and wine, which may be purchased but not consumed outside on the Wharf) as you walk. Many art, tee shirt, and souvenir shops also display their wares outside.[1] Both the food and the souvenirs are appetizers of sorts, leading the tourist along their pathways to the inside of the restaurant or shop.

Inside the shops one finds images from nature that have been carved, molded, cast, stuffed, and painted. Sea otters, sea lions, sea gulls, and fish appear in all the artistic media. They are for sale, portable markers that can be carried off-site, reproductions that authenticate the real thing. In the restaurants one again encounters nature, this time marinaded, under glass, or in a grand bouillabaisse.

In January of 1985 the city council voted to increase the fines for oral advertising or "barking" on the Wharf. According to a newspaper account (*Monterey Peninsula Herald* 1/15/85:27) "The policy of the city has been that such oral advertising is degrading and detracting from the native sounds which complement the wharf." The city feared that the barking would result in shouting matches on the Wharf, as concessionaires employed barkers to counter their rivals' barkers. While concessionaires claimed barking increased sales by 20 percent, the city raised the fines for a violation from $25 to $100. Today people offering a free taste of hot chowder stand in front of the counters, softly calling out to passersby to try it (another part of the garden of appetizers). Thus, the chowder servers act as soft-spoken barkers, a modified oral tradition.

Some years ago (1982) the city cracked down on retail fish outlets for selling sea lion food. The right to sell squid or mackerel to feed the sea creatures was reserved for bait and charter boat concessions. The sea lion snacks, trays selling for fifty cents, were among the biggest tourist attractions on the Wharf and the fish markets' simple solution was to remove the signs advertising it as sea lion food and let the people do whatever they wanted to with the fish pieces. An employee of the

Fig. 4–2. Old Fisherman's Grotto restaurant on Fisherman's Wharf (photo by M. Norkunas 1987).

Peninsula Fish Company said he fed the sea lions, who would come all the way up to his hand to get the food. "I don't understand [the city's rule]," he said. "This place is a wharf. We're not downtown Alvarado Street" (*Monterey Peninsula Herald* 10/13/82:21).

Disney-fying Nature

Just to the right of the Fisherman's Wharf entry sign may be found metal newspaper boxes and, in good weather, the monkey man. Some restaurant owners on Fisherman's Wharf complained to me about the monkey man, but the city, usually so strict about permitting anything on the Wharf that detracts from its "character," allows him to stay. It is a kind of street performance: the man plays some prerecorded music while a small costumed monkey takes the coins offered by children, often kissing the children in return. The monkey is trained, obviously the property of the man, and clothed in a little red suit reminiscent of outfits worn by black porters in old movies. The monkey man symbolizes the kind of relationship tourists are led to expect of man and nature on the Wharf. The attraction, a staged event, acts out the relationship which is re-presented throughout the Wharf: man's ability to tame and dominate nature; and nature as subservient, entertaining.

The man and nature relationship is again enacted at the opposite end of Fisherman's Wharf. Here the sea lions are the great attraction and here again they have come to represent colonized nature. The lions are migrating mammals and spend part of each year in the Monterey Bay. From the time when the quiet of the night settles until the commencement of the day, their barking can be heard many blocks from the sea. They know to congregate near the fishing boats and tourists on the Wharf, for here they are fed (and admired, if that matters to them). While they must compete with the pelicans and sea gulls for the pieces of chopped fish thrown to them, they have "learned" how to become adept performers. Like the monkey is his red coat and hat, the sea lions have become Disney-fied caricatures of themselves in nature. The sea life assumes the confectionary quality of Disneyland's Main Street, becoming more like what it ideally should be than what it actually is (Wallace 1989:162). The sea lions are wild, in nature, and yet they bark for food and jump out of the water as any trained dolphin from Seaworld might do.[2] On Fisherman's Wharf tourists ask if the sea lions are tame and where the restaurant owners put them at night. The animals appear as purposeful, organized entertainment for the benefit of the tourists.

This is a twist in the notion of a staged attraction. In this case tourists assume that an attraction has been staged, when it is actually a real or authentic encounter with nature. There has been yet another twist in the tourist/wildlife relationship. Pelicans, who normally make a stop in the Monterey Bay, snack on the fish close to the surface of the water, and migrate to warmer waters in Southern California and Mexico when the cold weather sets in, remained on Fisherman's Wharf in the winter of 1987–88. They had grown accustomed to the "recreational feeding" by tourists at the Wharf area. The food supply, however, left with the last of the tourists and the pelicans, who could no longer find food for themselves in nature, suffered from malnutrition, stress, and a disease brought on by these last two conditions. Their departure from nature and into domesticated attractions cost the pelican community three hundred members between 1987 and 1988.

Fig. 4–3. Tourists feeding sea lions and pelicans on Fisherman's Wharf (photo by M. Norkunas 1987).

People may also purchase a fishing experience from one of the fishing boat fleets. They rent all the necessary equipment, are taken out to sea, and do battle with nature, hopefully arriving back at the Wharf with a plentiful supply of good sized fish. Here the act of fishing, a major industry in the community, has been transformed into a saleable leisure activity. As a leisure activity the fishing is not done with nets, but rather with a fishing pole, to increase the challenge. Not only the place of work, but what was once (and still is) an act of work, fishing, has itself become a thing of leisure.

Marginalizing Ethnicity

The Fisherman's Wharf Association, an organization devoted to the interests of the businesses on the Wharf, is dominated by Italian-Amer-

Fig. 4–4. Sport Fishing and Street Artist on Fisherman's Wharf (photo by M. Norkunas 1987).

icans. The Italian-Americans have assumed somewhat of a monopoly on the Wharf. I once heard a rumor that a Middle Eastern man opened a restaurant on the Wharf and that it did not succeed because he was not Italian. One restaurant today is not Italian, and I did hear an Italian restaurateur remark that perhaps that man does not succeed because he is not Italian. The Italian ethnicity of the Wharf is not used as a marketing tool, nor does it serve as a marker for the Wharf. It is only apparent from the names of the restaurants and shops.

Not a five-minute walk from the Wharf are the bocci courts where, each sunny afternoon, men can be seen playing the game. The language of play is Italian. This is not a staged event, but people engaging in an actual ethnic leisure activity. The tourist literature, with rare exceptions, does not remark upon this aspect of local culture as site worthy.[3]

Peter Coniglio, a former mayor of the city, spoke of the insularity of the various ethnic groups in Monterey. He told me that Italians never integrated very well and consequently produced few community leaders. They remained close-knit and maintained their old ways. While non-Italians in Monterey viewed this ethnic community as one colony, they are actually bifurcated into Genovese Italian-Americans and Sicilian-Americans.

The Italian community, associated with fishing since their arrival in Monterey, had long held a festival to bless their fleet of fishing boats. When the fishing industry declined, so too did the importance of the festival. In 1970, as part of the Monterey bicentennial, twelve ethnic celebrations were held to illustrate the role that different ethnic groups played in the settlement of California and the history of Monterey (*Monterey Peninsula Herald* Supplement City of Monterey, 1970 Annual Report, 4/16/71). In the context of the bicentennial, the Santa Rosalia festival was redone on a larger scale with an outdoor mass, a procession, and a ride on the fleet. The festival has continued into the 1980s and, although it has changed since the early days of its enactment, it remains primarily for Italians. Only Italian food is served and it is not advertised outside of the Peninsula region.

In 1970 the Italian Heritage Society of the Monterey Peninsula erected a statue to Santa Rosalia, "Patron Saint of Italian Fishermen in Monterey." The statue stands to the left of Fisherman's Wharf, near the walking path to Cannery Row, and faces the harbor. The bronze plaque beneath it reads:

Santa Rosalia
Patron Saint of the Italian
Fishermen in Monterey
Palermo 1132—September 4, 1166
This monument is respectfully and gratefully
dedicated in memory of those courageous Sicilian
Fishermen whose labors and pioneering spirit
At the beginning of the 20th century
Created and Developed a Great Sardine Industry and
Whose Heritage and Culture Contributed Significantly
To the growth of this city and its surrounding areas

The Italian Heritage Society
Of the Monterey Peninsula
Monterey September 4, 1970

Some two hundred feet behind the statue of Santa Rosalia, nestled almost invisibly among trees and a small parking area, is another ethnic marker. This one is a bust of Pietro Ferrante, 1867–1954, who "By

Fig. 4–5. Statue of Santa Rosalia with Fisherman's Wharf in the background (photo by M. Norkunas 1987).

vision and example [was] an inspiration and leader among the founders of the Monterey Fishing and canning industry which added greatly to the history and fortune of Monterey." The monument was erected in the early 1970s from private family funds. Yet a third ethnic marker exists near, but not on, Fisherman's Wharf. It stands just outside the large parking area leading into the Wharf. It is a bronze plaque honoring a man named Shedo "Buck" Russo, one of only two Italian mayors in Monterey. Buck Russo was mayor from 1959–1961 (Peter Coniglio served from 1973–1977). The plaque reads:

Shedo S. "Buck" Russo
"Citizen of Monterey"
Mayor 1959–1961
Councilman—1941–1959
The Council and the City of Monterey Proudly
And Gratefully Dedicates to the Memory of
Shedo S. "Buck" Russo—Citizen of Monterey—This

Marina in Recognition of His Many Years of
Devoted Service to the City He Loved and
So Ably Represented
October 12, 1971

A fourth monument, erected by the Fisherman's Wharf Association, rests at the intersection of six main streets. There are no pedestrian paths leading to it, nor any place to stop a car. It is a boat called the Santa Maria, and while it is very visible from a car, its significance is less easy to determine without an opportunity to examine it more closely. The accompanying bronze plaque (not visible from a car) reads:

This Harbor is the home of....
Monterey's Commercial Fishing Fleet.
It once boasted the largest
Sardine Fishing Industry in the world.
An industry that flourished until the late 1940s.
Commercial fishing was pioneered and developed here
By Sicilian fishermen, whose courage and vision
Contributed significantly to
The history and culture of Monterey.
Our bay continues to rank as one of the
Major fishing areas on the west coast.

The "Santa Maria" is an original Monterey-style boat
With her distinctive bow and rounded stern.
Designed for these waters, This type of vessel is
Internationally known as a "Double-Ender."
She was built in 1918 and skippered by three generations
of the Sal of Franco family
Who fished this Bay from the turn of the century.

The Fisherman's Wharf Association purchased the
"Santa Maria" in 1975 and, in conjunction with
the city of Monterey, Created this living tribute
to the members of those gallant fishermen who played
Such an important role in the economic and spiritual growth
of the beautiful Monterey Bay area.
Dedicated in 1978.

All of the monuments were erected in the 1970s, a time when the country was experiencing an interest in minority and ethnic history. Locally, the Italian-Americans were in a position to achieve parity with the structure of power that dominated the city's politics, as evidenced by Peter Coniglio's election as mayor. As the Italians achieved political power, they engaged in the process of erecting public markers to themselves. The circumstances that allowed Coniglio to be elected mayor also permitted the city of Monterey, the Italian Heritage Society, the family of Pietro Ferrante (a relative of Coniglio), and the Fisherman's Wharf Association to erect this series of public markers.

The monuments are significant moments of "Otherness" (Dorst 1989:180), full of a density of meaning that resists the touristic process of stylization and reduction to a simple codified history. They stand in stark contrast to the official history's sense of exploration and conquest.

The Italian monuments instead use their inscriptions to tell a local history of Italian contributions to the industry and culture of Monterey. They carry such words as courage, vision, inspiration, devoted service, heritage and culture, and describe Italians as contributors to both the economic and spiritual growth of the Monterey Bay area. The imagery chosen to represent the Italians includes a male figure of industry and invention (Pietro Ferrante is credited with introducing the lampara net to Monterey and revolutionizing the fishing industry); a male figure of politics (Russo); a female figure from the cosmology of Italian fishermen, who acted as their protector (Santa Rosalia); and a work vessel, a Monterey style boat. Both the imagery and the inscriptions are unlike the historic houses found in other parts of Monterey's system of public history. They represent a glimpse of a broader, more multifaceted system: they offer themselves up as symbols of work, religion, industry and politics.

Like Steinbeck's cannery workers, his migrant workers, and his paisanos, the statuary represent instances in which ethnic or class minorities have publicly and symbolically affirmed their identities in the city. Unlike the cannery workers, the Italian presence in Monterey did not disappear with the closing of the canneries and, thus, could not be reduced to the caricaturization that the workers Steinbeck described were to undergo. Instead, the statuary was marginalized. The monuments' physical placement on the landscape is a metaphor for the Italian relationship to structures of power. Like the creators' tenuous hold on political power,[4] the monuments are tenuous, not in their construction but in their location. Like the ethnic minorities in Monterey, the monuments are set apart from the mainstream pedestrian paths, hidden under trees, or placed in an impossible-to-reach intersection.

The notion of site de-sacralization applies to the statuary. Unlike the marking that identifies Fisherman's Wharf as a site worthy of preservation, the momuments are symbolically represented on the landscape as nonsites. No easy access or obvious signposts mark the monuments, and, in the case of the Santa Maria, access is difficult if not impossible. The statue of Pietro Ferrante is not set apart from the parking lot where it resides, not elevated or otherwise bounded.

Italians were permitted to erect public reminders of their own cultures, which did not challenge the structure of domination in Monterey society. Nature also resists domination, as evidenced by the contrived "wildness" of the pelicans and sea lions. History, ethnicity, and nature are made safe so that the tourist can experience all three minimally, free to consume such experiences, along with a multitude of consumer goods, in an environment of unreflective leisure.

Notes

1. When once I commented to Rich Hughett, Public Relations Director for the Fisherman's Wharf Association, that the wharf had a multitude of souvenir shops, he hurridly corrected me saying that while they existed he had also purchased some beautiful artwork on the wharf. Moreover, he went on to say, the Monterey sweatshirts he had sent to his relatives in the northern climates had been greatly appreciated.
2. One flashes for a moment to the soft furry creatures walking around Disneyland, a five-foot chipmunk holding someone's hand, or Cinderella on film singing to (and being sung to by) the birds and the mice. One ranger from Yellowstone National Park complained that people had been so influenced by the fictious animals in Disney's films that they approach real bears in nature thinking that they would be as cute and loving as Walt Disney's bears.
3. This lack of touristic interest in the bocci games may ultimately act to protect the local people from ethnic tourism referred to earlier, in which insiders become what they believe tourists think they are, resulting in a freezing of ethnic imagery in which the host becomes a caricature of him or herself (MacCannell 1984; Van den Berghe and Keyes 1984). I am not arguing to use ethnicity as a marketing tool, but instead to seek that delicate balance in which ethnicity is recognized without being exploited.
4. The Italian tenure of office was short: rumors circulated in Mon-

terey about Italian involvement in the construction of the controversial Monterey Sheraton Hotel. The hotel, considered by many townspeople as an eyesore, and a revision of the plans originally submitted and approved by the town, is said to have cost certain political figures their jobs.

5

❖ ❖ ❖

Public History, Tourist Landscapes, and the Reconfiguration of Reality: Concluding Thoughts

❖ ❖ ❖ ❖ ❖

My approach to tourism was initially grounded in my interest in authenticity. I searched out the ways in which tourist sites, as products of postmodern consumer culture, used a complex system of messages to authenticate themselves. After a short time in the field, I came to see that authenticity only explained small portions of the cultural texts created by the city of Monterey. The most general way to accurately describe these texts is the politics of public memory. These texts, I came to see, had not been marshalled out of the reality of the city, but had been selectively constructed to affirm a particular ideology. Certain groups in the city claimed their power was based on social evolutionary superiority and substantiated that claim through distortions in historical and touristic texts. History, literature, ethnicity, class, nature, and even industrialism were brought under control and integrated into the ideology of dominance.

The cultural texts on tourism were concentrated in three geographical regions of the city. These three regions I identified as the principal tourist sites in Monterey: the Path of History, Cannery Row, and Fisherman's Wharf. They offered themselves up as three distinct areas of analysis, yet they could also be seen as one grand cultural production that resonated with hegemonic themes. It took many readings of these sites to go beyond a literal interpretation. If hegemony, dominance, authenticity, and the politics of public memory were my larger texts, then class, ethnicity, nature, history, the literary landscape, and economics as played out in the transformation from industrialism to postindustrialism were subtexts. In each of the sites, the subtexts related to each other in particular ways, so that on Fisherman's Wharf, for example, ethnicity, nature, and history formed a unique typology. Yet in every site these texts and subtexts communicated similar messages.

Markers, or signs indicating actual sites, are to be found on the Path of History, on Cannery Row, and on Fisherman's Wharf. The signs help the tourists to determine the character of a place, to understand what makes Paris Paris, or what makes Monterey Monterey. They indicate which sections of the city are presented for tourists to see, which houses in Old Monterey are site-worthy, what one should do on Fisherman's Wharf and where one should eat on Cannery Row (from the off-site marker, the travel brochure).

I paid particular attention to the markers that framed each of my sites, looking especially for "sentries" guarding the entrances. At the Monterey city line stands the suggestion of a fence laden with the emblems of the sanctioned civic organizations; at the Larkin House on the Path of History the tour guide acts as a local history "gatekeeper"; the monkey man and the anchor guard the entry to Fisherman's Wharf. Canneries, transformed into elite cultural and touristic institutions, stand at either end of Cannery Row, combining metaphors for social class, dominance, and nature. The buildings stand firm against any efforts at reminiscence about bygone days of industrialism and later poverty. All of the "sentries" convey political and cultural messages about power and ideology.

There is a consistent lack of recognition of various social classes and ethnic groups in all three of the sites. This exclusion from the historical record and from the tourist landscape is covert. In the Path of History's Pacific House, Native Americans and Mexicans are captured in the ethnographic present; they are rarely mentioned on the rest of the Path. Cannery Row's fame as a street is based on industrial canneries that were made famous by the literature of John Steinbeck. The city's historical organizations did not concern themselves with this historical period and the tourist industry reduced Steinbeck's social commentary to caricature. Apart from this, the ethnic and class history of the Row is ignored. Fisherman's Wharf, dominated by Italians, has the most complicated relationship with the topic of ethnicity. Ethnic statuary and monuments are found near the Wharf, but they have been physically marginalized so that they merely touch the periphery of the tourist trails.

Portrayals of nature exhibit this same sense of cultural domination. Like history, aspects of nature are selected, constructed, controlled, and modelled into displays. Canneries, which once processed fish, now display them as biological curiosities (the aquarium) or offer them up as leisure displays (hotels offering diving experiences to tourists). Fishing boats take tourists out on whale watching expeditions, or on pleasure fishing trips. The tourists who congregate to see the sea lions and pelicans on Fisherman's Wharf think of them as tame, existing for their pleasure, while the monkey man bespeaks a colonial relationship with nature.

A subtle but forceful blending of reality and fantasy is to be found in each of the three sites. This is most apparent on Cannery Row, where markers will be placed on actual sites as well as on the places that existed only in Steinbeck's imagination. The reproduction comes to transcend the real so that the Row is legitimated in so far as it offers participation in the fictionalized landscape created by Steinbeck. Steinbeck's fiction, in turn, only becomes acceptable to the tourist landscape when it has been redigested, caricatured. The interplay between the real and the pseudo on Fisherman's Wharf takes the form of a staged quality, giving a Disney-like appearance to nature when, in fact, it is real. The Path of History offers temporal examples of the comingling of reality and fantasy, as aspects of the past are selectively brought forward and imaginatively reproduced.

Each of these subtexts is derived from an array of physical structures and objects and from site-specific social systems. A historic home is not only the building itself, but the furniture it contains, the marker announcing that the house is noteworthy, the guided tour that occurs within it, the tourist literature that describes it, and the group(s) of people who cause the house to be seen as valuable. It is partially through this manipulation of artifacts that value is socially created. The powerful amass an array of artifacts that purport to tell the actual story of the past. Through this process these artifacts become socially valued. They in turn actually portray a selective history that legitimizes the values of that ruling class.

This process is effectively described by Michael Thompson's rubbish theory. All of the sites had structures that had become devalued to the point where demolition was a real possibility, and all were rescued to varying degrees from their valueless state and became valuable. Fisherman's Wharf was to be demolished when it lost its function after the commercial fishing wharf was built. Instead, it became a leisure-oriented facsimile of a new "real" fishing wharf. Cannery Row's canneries were abandoned, sometimes intentionally burned, before they leapt into prominence as transformed reminders of both the reconstructed past and Steinbeck's fictionalized version of that past. The Cooper-Molera Adobe on the Path of History was in ruins when it was deemed worthy of restoration by the state and suddenly became significant enough to receive two million dollars in restoration funds. Historical minitexts stand in front of the now valued sites on Fisherman's Wharf and the houses on the Path of History, enshrining them and, hence, protecting them from being physically destroyed or popularly ignored and thus devalued. Other sites remain as rubbish. Some are real rubbish—the worker housing on Cannery Row which is unable to move into a valued state—and some are pseudo rubbish—the rusted boilers for the proposed park on Cannery Row, which were to have been cleaned and set upon a grassy knoll.

Each of the sites is involved in the reconfiguration of reality. In the case of tourism, that reconfigured reality is overtly aimed at the outsider, who, for a number of reasons has come to involve him or herself in one or all of the three sites. More importantly, the past has been reconstructed and reality reconfigured to convince (more covertly) insiders in the community that this is history, their reality. Yet these insiders are conspirators, in a sense, in creating their past and present public identities. The creators and consumers of the tourist landscapes represent the two-sidedness of hegemony, the popular consent to domination. A kind of accepted notion is created as the governing class overcomes its own narrow interests and forms a bloc with other classes and class fragments. As Linda Nochlin pointed out in her analysis of women, art, and power:

> It is important to keep in mind that one of the most important functions of ideology is to veil the overt power relations obtaining in society at a particular moment in history by making them appear to be part of the natural eternal order of things. It is also important to remember that symbolic power is invisible and can be exercised only with the complicity of those who fail to recognize either that they submit to it or that they exercise it (Nochlin 1988:2).

The ruling class carefully controls the form and content of historical re-creations and tourist landscapes, legitimizing itself by projecting its own contemporary sociocultural values upon the past. This struggle, the tension between groups with power and groups with varying but lesser degrees of power, is replayed in the many spheres in which the public enactment of identity is staged. The erection or nonerection of statuary and the placement of that statuary is a physical manifestation of that tension; nostalgic reinterpretations of socially condemnatory fiction, which results in a humorous caricature of poverty is yet another manifestation of the struggle. Dominance is expressed not in terms of physical coercion but as rhetoric.

> But if there is a single, overriding quality of postmodern hegemony, it is that dominance becomes almost entirely a matter of texts or images, of the rhetorical deployment of discourse practices. One corollary of this fact is that postmodern hegemony has the potential of penetrating more deeply and colonizing more completely every sphere of experience than those orders of dominance that require visible forces of coercion and external control to sustain themselves (Dorst 1989:176).

Yet there are contradictions, instances that resist hegemonic codification. John Steinbeck's literature exists in a permanent form, however much it has been altered on Cannery Row; the Italian statuary stands, regardless of its marginality; a Mexican portion of a historic home has been interpreted, even if incompletely; and, despite their Disneylike actions, the sea lions and pelicans remain wild.

What could have taken place in this city? There could have been a recognition of the ways in which the values and cultures of its inhabitants had shaped its present identity. A series of questions could be raised as to how the particular experience of Monterey's past is related to a broader systemic perspective regarding ethnicity, industrialism, social class, nature, and the relations between them. Difficult issues could be addressed directly: did the Spanish settlement of Monterey destroy the Native American community? Was Father Serra a saint or a sinner? What was the relationship between the Spanish inhabitants of Monterey and the Mexican residents? How did the city change when Mexico seceded from Spain and ruled California? What kinds of relationships existed between the Native Americans and the Spanish and Mexicans?

A penetrating analysis of the Vallejo family would offer rich insights into the social and political structure of the Mexican period. This would go far beyond the current one dimensional portrait of Mexican culture in the city's historical sites. A systematic study of the changing experiences of ordinary people, including ordinary Mexicans, would create a strong linkage between the past and the present (Blewett 1989:263). As one critic suggested, the recreated home of a Mexican family would offer rich interpretive opportunities.

The city's economic past might also be explored in a more thoughtful way. One of the city's major sources of revenue, the canneries is nearly absent from the public history texts.

The whole industrial era could be investigated. Who ran the canneries? Were they unionized? What kinds of labor issues arose? How did deindustrialization or, as Michael Wallace refers to it, the global reorganization of capitalism, impact the demise of the canneries? What happened to the former cannery workers?

The involvement of the Portuguese, Italian, and Japanese communities in the past and present history of Monterey could be pursued. Oral histories could be actively conducted by qualified professionals to collect the memoirs of the various ethnic communities. These could direct the construction of public exhibitory. Academics engaged in the new social history could be employed as consulting professionals, linking critical thinking on the city's past with the public presentation of that history.

The two active historical organizations in the city, the Monterey History and Art Association and the Monterey State Historic Park, could enlarge their scopes of interest to include the twentieth century and the various ethnic communities and classes who lived and live in Monterey. They might form advisory groups composed of representatives from the various ethnic groups to recommend public history projects.

The commercial tourist areas might seek to become more (rather than less, as is the current tendency) sensitive to their historic landscapes. It may, in fact, be in their best economic interest to insist on a sense of place that is rooted in the city's real past. Without attempting to sell Italians as exotic local culture, some mention might be made of special Italian regional dishes in the restaurants. Written materials could include selections from Italian immigrant narratives. The same might be done for the Portuguese community and other ethnic communities.

As a practitioner of public history, I know only too well that these suggestions could not be easily implemented. But the effort to acknowledge ethnic and class diversity will be noticed by visitors and, more importantly, by those very "multicultural" audiences whose histories have been institutionally ignored.

Ethnic and class groups have not forgotten the totality of their own pasts. They have certainly preserved a sense of themselves through orally transmitted family stories, and through celebrations and rituals performed inside the group. But their systematic exclusion from official history fragments the community so that feelings of alienation and 'loss of soul' are experienced most deeply by minorities.

What is needed is an acknowledgement that power must be shared with minority populations and that the prevailing perspective on the past must be radically altered. Human's relationship with nature must be reexamined, especially as that relationship is portrayed in the tourist landscape. The changing economic structure of the community must be thoughtfully analyzed, especially as it relates to a changing national economy. The community must then have the courage to enact these new insights on the public landscapes of history and tourism.

APPENDIX:
SITE DESCRIPTIONS OF
THE PATH OF HISTORY

❖　❖　❖　❖　❖

Brief Descriptions of Selected Structures on the Path of History

The First Brick House (owned by the Monterey State Historic Park, closed for restoration). Partially built in 1846 by Gallant G. Dickenson, who had come "overland" to California, the house was abandoned when Dickenson joined the Gold Rush. It was the first brick house built in California and was undergoing restoration in the mid-1980s. When it is completed it will be operated by the Junior League of Monterey County.

The Old Whaling Station (owned by the Monterey State Historic Park, open one day per week). Built in the 1840s as a private home for David Wight, a Scottish born architect, it became a boardinghouse for Portuguese whalers in the 1850s. The State of California and the Junior League of Monterey County renovated the building and the Junior League is leasing it.

The Viscaino, Portola and Serra Landing Site Originally a sandy beach, the cove was buried under landfill from the construction of the railroad to Pacific Grove. The Spanish explorer Sebastian Viscaino landed at the beach in 1602. On June 3, 1770 Don Gaspar de Portola and Father Junipero Serra arrived at the site and claimed California for the King of Spain. The site is adjacent to a busy street and, as no pedestrian path is provided, access is difficult.

The Mayo Hayes O'Donnell Library (owned by the Monterey History and Art Association, open several afternoons per week). Built in 1876, this building was the first Protestant church erected in Monterey.

Threatened with destruction by urban renewal, the Monterey History and Art Association moved it to its present location in 1970. It now houses a library of California history, much of which was donated by Mayo Hayes O'Donnell from her private collection. O'Donnell was a member of the Monterey History and Art Association and also donated Casa Soberanes to the State of California.

The Francis Doud House (owned by the Monterey History and Art Association, houses the association's costume collection). Irish-born Francis Doud came to Monterey in July 1848 with his wife and son. He served as a civilian employee for the governor and worked on the physical arrangements of the California Constitutional Convention. In 1860 he built his home and there entertained friends from all walks of life. The Monterey History and Art Association acquired the house in 1969 to preserve it in the face of urban renewal and as an example of a local wooden house in the Early American period. The gardens (original?) surrounding the house were dedicated as the Carmel Martin Memorial Garden in 1973. The house is not presently open to the public.

The First Theatre (owned by the Monterey State Historic Park, the theatre is operated by the Troupers of the Gold Coast who perform melodramas each weekend). Jack Swan, an English sailor, built a saloon and apartment house in the 1840s. When the Mexican War ended, soldiers persuaded him to erect a stage and began to perform melodramas. The house was packed the first night of the performance. The California Historic Landmarks League and the citizens of Monterey purchased the building and gave it to the State of California in 1906. The theatre is open daily for lunch and dinner and for the weekend melodramas.

Casa Soberanes (owned by the Monterey State Historic Park, the house is open six days per week for tours). The house, sometimes known as "The House with the Blue Gate," was originally built in the 1840s by Rafael Estrada, the half brother of Governor Juan Alvarado. Two generations of Soberanes owned the adobe house. It was restored in the 1920s and given to the State of California in the 1950s by its then owner, Mayo Hayes O'Donnell and her husband, a writer for the *Monterey Peninsula Herald*. The house is presented as a unique blending of the architecture of Southern Spain and New England and its furnishings reflect a blend of China trade pieces, Mexican folk art, and New England items. It is a two-story, thick walled adobe with a cantilevered balcony with no posts to support the roof. The roof slants from its two-story height in the front to a single-story height in the rear, with upper floor rooms placed along the front only. The "sala" or living room has been used as an example of early adobe by the Thorne collection of miniature rooms in the Chicago Art Institute. The house is often cited as one of the Path of History's few Mexican or Spanish style homes. The interior of the house, however, has been kept as it looked when its last owners, the Hayes O'Donnells, lived there.

Colton Hall (owned by the City of Monterey, it is open daily). The Reverend Walter Colton, who arrived in Monterey as a chaplain on one of Commodore Sloat's vessels, was appointed to serve as alcalde or Chief Magistrate of the Monterey district. He held this position from 1846 until 1849. He also published the first newspaper in California on August 15, 1846. During this period he directed the construction of the first American public building based on the labor of convicts, taxes from town lots and liquor shops, and fines on gamblers. The building has been in continuous use as a public office building since that time. It was in Colton Hall that the California Constitutional Convention was held in 1849 and it is for this reason that the building has been made into a museum. The second floor houses a permanent exhibit showing a re-creation of the papers and desks that the convention delegates must have used. This exhibit is referred to as "living history." The City of Monterey and the Museum Board restored the building in 1949. The Monterey State Historic Park's General Plan states, under acquisitions, that should the city ever decide to sell the building, it is a priority for the state to acquire. A guide, paid for by the city, is available on a daily basis to answer questions. The museum also has a full-time director, who serves on a number of community cultural committees.

The Allen Knight Maritime Museum (owned by the Monterey History and Art Association, open six days per week, staffed by volunteer Watchstanders; the building also houses the offices of the Monterey History and Art Association). The museum opened in 1971 under the sponsorship of the Monterey History and Art Association. It houses the personal collection of maritime artifacts and relics accumulated by Allen Knight of Carmel (who lived in a house decorated to resemble a ship). Since its opening, the museum has added many items to its collection. The collection includes, among its other artifacts, sailing ship models and navigation instruments, thousands of ship pictures, a model of Commodore Drake's flagship from his capture of Monterey in 1846, and a reproduction of a captain's cabin. The museum is composed of three rooms, with the first being a receiving room and book-shop. In the next room is a collection of Chinese junks, the Fresno Light from the Point Sur lighthouse, a short history of the sardine industry in Monterey, and many models of ships. To reach the third room, one walks down a long hall with paintings on its walls. The room houses paintings, ship models, and the captain's room. With many retired seamen from the Naval postgraduate school as volunteers (Watchmen), the museum's orientation is primarily maritime rather than local history. Some local history, however, is presented, such as a survey of the sardine industry and models of Chinese junks.

Casa Amesti (owned by the National Trust for Historic Preservation). Cited as one of the best examples of Monterey Colonial architecture, it was the home of José Amesti, son-in-law of Don José Vallejo. Leased by the National Trust for Historic Preservation to the Old Capitol Club for use as a private men's club, the building is open to the public for several hours every weekend.

Casa Gutierrez (owned by the Monterey State Historic Park and presently operated as a Mexican restaurant under a concession agreement). This was the home of Joaquin Gutierrez who came to Monterey from Mexico as a soldier in the 1830s, married into the old Escobar family, and raised fifteen children. The home has been called "typical of those of average citizens in Monterey during the Mexican period," but one must remember that the Escobar family was well known and of a certain social class. The adobe was preserved from a sale for taxes by the Monterey Foundation and purchased by the State of California in June of 1954. Because it is a restaurant, the public section of the house has not been interpreted.

The Stevenson House (owned by the State of California, the house is open six days per week). The original portion of the building dates from the 1830s and was the home of Don Rafael Gonzales, the first administrator of customs for Alta, or Upper California. Later Juan Girardin, called by some publications Swiss and by others French (he was probably a French-speaking Swiss), bought the house and added on to it. He and his wife rented spare bedrooms to roomers, among them Robert Louis Stevenson, who occupied an upstairs bedroom for three months in 1879. Stevenson wrote *The Old Pacific Capital* while staying in Monterey. He had come here to be near Fanny Osbourne, whom he married a few months later. The house had served many purposes and was for a time known as the "French Hotel." The late Edith

C. van Antwerp and Mrs. C. Tobin Clark purchased the adobe in 1937 to save it from destruction and presented it to the State of California as a memorial. It serves as a repository for Stevensoniana, acting as a kind of artifactual biography. The first floor is full of items once belonging to Stevenson, including photographs of his days in Samoa, and furniture given to Stevenson and Fanny Osbourne by Stevenson's parents in Scotland. One of the rooms upstairs purports to represent Stevenson's bedroom as it was when he lived in it. According to the guide, the house is one of four Stevenson museums in the world, the others being in Napa Valley, New York, and Scotland. Again, according to the guide, the house is not meant to show Stevenson's life but rather to house Stevenson artifacts, although a guided tour through the artifacts does reveal a great deal about the author's life. It is in no way representative of the house as it was when Stevenson lived there. Upstairs, in addition to Stevenson's bedroom, are rooms full of Victorian artifacts—a kind of open storage of the gifts given to the State of California.

The Joseph Boston Store (owned by the Monterey State Historic Park and staffed by volunteer members of the Monterey History and Art Association). Built by Thomas Larkin as a business structure in the 1840s, the building was sold to José Abrego, who leased it to Joseph Boston and Company in the 1850s for a mercantile business. The building became known as Casa del Oro as a result of the story that it had been a gold depository for the miners returning from the California gold rush. David Jack later bought the structure and used it as a storehouse and private home. It was given to the State of California by the Jack sisters and opened as a store again in April 1985. Today its shelves are stocked with antiques, ribbons, linens, crockery, tea, books, and other articles in keeping with materials that could have been purchased in the mid-nineteenth century store. The shop also features herbs grown in the adjoining garden and descriptions of their use in early California.

Detailed Descriptions of the Custom House
and the Cooper-Molera Adobe

The Custom House (owned by the Monterey State Historic Park, open daily). Built about 1827 by the Mexican government, this is the oldest government building on the Pacific Coast. As the name implies, it served as a custom house from the 1820s, when Mexico opened the port of Monterey to foreign trade, until 1867. The interior was used to unload cargo from the incoming ships and assess duties. It was also the setting for social occasions. It was at the Custom House that Commodore John Drake Sloat declared California a part of the United States on July 7, 1846. Landmark status had been sought for the building in the 1880s, but it was not until 1900 that the Native Sons of the Golden West managed to lease it from the U.S. Treasury Department for one dollar per year. In 1903 the State of California took over the lease and provided funds for restoration. It again provided restoration funds in 1917. In 1929 the Custom House was opened to the public and in 1938, with matching funds provided by local citizens, the state park's system acquired the building.

The building is located near the shoreline and the entrance to Fisherman's Wharf. Few of the people walking down the road that connects the parking area to the Wharf stop and enter the Custom House (which is the only State building on the Path of History that is free of charge. Other buildings require a one dollar entry fee). This may be due in part to the fact that the entry sign is small, the thick adobe walls cause the inside to look dark, and it is not entirely apparent that the building is open to the public. To the right of the Custom House is a large plaza (the Custom House Plaza) and behind it another large open space. Craft fairs and other public events are often held in these open plazas. The second large plaza is bordered on one side by the Pacific House. Custom House Plaza features a bandstand, benches, and the bocci courts.

In the small entry room of the Custom House are glass cases on the walls. These contain a chronological and thematic exhibit of the history of the building. The exhibit consists of seven displays and a glassed-in model of a ship in the center of the room (The Brig Pilgrim 1835). Each display case has a quote from a trader in California—William Henry Dana, Commodore Sloat, Thomas Larkin—and a painting, drawing, or photograph, and several artifacts. The first case describes the people of Monterey's interest in the goods on a cargo ship and shows a man and a woman in Mexican-style dress. Products of New England and European factories were exchanged for cowhides and tallow, the display states. The second case shows men unloading cargo from a ship, has a map of trade routes and explains how the Custom House collected cargo duties for Mexico. The third display case is a

Fig. A–1. Custom House exterior (photo by M. Norkunas 1987).

night scene, depicting men unloading cargo at Yerba Buena or other points, saying that invoices were arranged to suit the plans of merchants. There follows a framed drawing of the harbor and city of Monterey, circa 1842, and another display case. This is meant to portray Sloat's landing and states that California's simple pastoral life underwent considerable change with the advent of the American occupation of 1846. The next display case is a collage of photos of the Custom House. Adjacent to it is a case with a line drawing of a Mexican man and a ship's captain in front of goods in a room. It reads in part "Come step back into time and see how it may have appeared on a day in the 1830s when a ship's cargo was being declared."

The second room is very large and represents the contents of a ship circa 1840. The display used a ship's manifest along with *Two Years Before the Mast* (William Henry Dana's mid-1800s account of life on board a trading ship off the coast of California and his observations of the cultures of the native peoples he visited) to determine what items a trading vessel might have unloaded into the Custom House. All items from ships entering the harbor were once unloaded into the Custom House and a 100 percent duty was imposed. The ship was then free to trade along the coast of California (interviews with Monterey State Historic Park guides 10/6/87; 10/27/87). While the room itself is somewhat dark, the multitude of items displayed creates a colorful ambiance. The cargo includes a live parrot, boxes and crates marked with their imagined port of origin, cloth goods, tin products hanging from the ceiling, and glass and chinaware. Sugar, pressed into cones, is displayed to show how it was transported from Mexico; cowhides once called California Bank Notes, are piled up at the end of a long table.

The third room resembles a dining room. Upstairs a bedroom, roped off so that visitors stay only at the entry, is displayed. There are no written explanations of these rooms and the guides confined their talks to the cargo room.

The Custom House is meant to capture the visitors' interest so that they will go on to see the other buildings on the Path of History. The Custom House and the Pacific House, unlike many of the other houses on the Path, do not offer organized tours of their interiors. Rather, guides are available to answer questions, although they often end up by giving prepared tours.

On my first trip to the Custom House the guide explained to me that approximately two ships a month unloaded their cargo in that very room, where it was inspected and charged according to what the customs official wanted. If, however, the custom inspector was a friend of the ship's captain then the cargo would not have to be unloaded from the ship, but was inspected right on board. The guide implied that payoffs may have occurred. She mentioned that all objects in the room were a re-creation and pointed out several features that had not been duplicated: the floor was probably hard-packed adobe and not wood as it is today, it would have been dirtier, and things (lamps, utentils) would probably not have been hung from the ceiling. The preparation, commercial uses, trade value and economic importance of cowhides and sugar cones, popular attractions with school groups who visit the building, were explained at some length.

The second time I toured the building (approximately three weeks later) I was given a somewhat different story by the ranger stationed at the Custom House that day. She was appalled that the first guide should have implied graft on the part of the customs inspector, saying that such comments "confirm suspicions about the worst of Mexicans."

This woman made a special effort to praise things Hispanic, both Spanish and Mexican, saying that many of the children who visit the Custom House are Hispanic and that it is also our background (our meaning people from the area). She, too, pointed out the sugar cones and mentioned that sugar is still transported that way from Mexico to Gonzales (a town in Northern California). Quoting from Dana she praised the Mexicans' moderate use of alcohol, their fine horsemanship, and explained some of their habits as derivative of a culture based on leisure. Pointing out the contradictions in the room, she indicated that the cowhides did not really belong there for they would more likely be found on a ship leaving California to export local goods, rather than a ship entering the harbor.

The Custom House, as a building located solidly in Monterey's Mexican period, appears to be organized around the theme of trade. It describes traded items, through the unloaded cargo ship, in a colorful and interesting way. Yet the fact that Mexicans created and maintained the building and the business is not well articulated. When Mexican life is presented, it is referred to as California's simple pastoral life (how California was before the American presence). Even the tour guide who strove to be sensitive to the Hispanic past could only cite Dana's description of the Mexican culture of leisure, for lack of other available, less biased literature.

The Cooper-Molera Adobe (leased from the National Trust for Historic Preservation by the Monterey State Historic Park, open to the public six days per week. The Old Monterey Preservation Society runs a museum store in the adobe complex). Captain John Rogers Cooper, an Englishman, trader, and sea captain, settled in Monterey in the 1820s and married Encarnación Vallejo, daughter of the prominent Mexican family. Taking the name of Juan Bautista Rogerio Cooper, he became a Mexican citizen and joined the Catholic Church. He built his home as a long one-story structure and by the 1850s had converted the southern section to the two-story building that exists today. Later, he planted an orchard, erected large barns, and added several small buildings in back of the house, all enclosed by a high adobe wall. Cooper sold the northern half section of his long house in 1933 to a stranger— the U.S. Consul to the Sandwich Islands. Ownership of that section changed hands several times. After 1845 it became the longtime home of Doña Luisa Estrada de Diaz, whose husband had established a business on Polk Street (the same street where the adobe stands). She lived continuously in the house longer than any other person or family. Manuel Diaz was alcalde (mayor) of Monterey when the Americans took possession of the area. He subsequently lost that position to Colton, and by 1855 was bankrupt—a fate many Mexicans experienced after the American takeover. In 1864 the Cooper family moved to San Francisco, where Captain Cooper died of influenza eight years later. Anna Cooper Wohler bought back the other portion of the house in 1902, reuniting the complex after a seventy-year split. In 1968 Cooper's granddaughter, Frances Molera, willed the walled-in complex to the National Trust for Historic Preservation.

The information presented above came from written sources. The two tours I took of the building revealed different information. During the first tour, the guide explained something about how Cooper had arrived in Monterey, and how the house had been willed to the National Trust by Cooper's granddaughter. The granddaughter was involved in the preservation decisions. The complex has been restored, at a cost of two million dollars, and continues to be worked on. It was decided to restore the house to the 1850s period because most of the furniture dated from that time. When Cooper was cash poor, and most of the guides spoke of Cooper's poor business sense, he sold half of his house. This would explain what to me was a puzzle in the written literature about the Cooper-Molera—why a wealthy man would sell part of his home to strangers.

The guide pointed out that the kitchens would have been outside at the time for fear of fire and to prevent excessive heat in the house, although now the kitchen is shown inside the house. The upstairs had been restored to represent Cooper's life in the mid-1800s.

When we went into the second part of the house, the section Cooper would have sold and which has purportedly been restored to resemble what it would have been like when Diaz lived there, the guide sensitively pointed out to me the contradictions she saw. The furniture was Victorian, which was unrealistic since a Mexican woman would have lived here. The bedroom was set up as a Mexican family would have decorated it: the bed in white linens and a woven grass mat on the floor. Other artifacts were not in character with a Mexican house, including the kinds of drinking vessels portrayed and the furniture in the entry room. She explained to me that Diaz had been an important Mexican shopkeeper, but when the United States took over California he lost his status.

On my second tour I first saw a slide show about the reconstruction of the Cooper-Molera. On the tour the guide (a different guide than I had had on the first tour) spoke of the history of the house and the problem of how to present a complex of buildings. She mentioned that people are put off by the fact that the buildings are new looking, but it appears as it would have when Cooper finished remodelling it. Unlike the first tour, when I was the sole visitor, this group was composed of seven persons. We went through the house room by room. In the upstairs portion the guide explained the reproduction of the original wallpaper in the *sala* or living room, the desk made to look as it would have when Cooper did his 1863 taxes, the table set with china from his China trade, the music room where guests would have seen the bear and bull fights outside, and the paintings Cooper would have purchased in San Francisco. Everything, she indicated, was original to the house, or purchased by the State to make the house complete. She did not comment on the Diaz house and its European furnishings. Mention was made on this tour, as it was on my first tour, of Cooper's relation to Larkin. They were half-brothers and it was Cooper who had requested Larkin travel west to assist him with his business affairs. While John Cooper never attained the political or economic importance of Thomas Larkin, he did enjoy a certain status in the community, at least according to the tour guides. The house is referred to as the Cooper-Molera Adobe, named after Cooper and his descendants, rather than the Cooper-Diaz Adobe, which would have recognized the long time residence of Doña Luisa Estrada de Diaz.

BIBLIOGRAPHY

❖ ❖ ❖ ❖ ❖

Abrahams, Roger D. 1986. Ordinary and Extraordinary Experience. In *The Anthropology of Experience*, eds. Victor W. Turner and Edward M. Bruner, pp. 45–72. Urbana: University of Illinois Press.

Aiken, Charles S. 1977. Faulkner's Yoknapatawpha County: Geographical Fact into Fiction. *The Geographical Review* 67:1–21.

Anderson, Jay. 1984. *Time Machines, The World of Living History*. Nashville, Tennessee: The American Association of State and Local History.

Ben-Amos, Dan. 1976. Analytical Categories and Ethnic Genres. In *Ethnic Genres*, ed. Dan Ben-Amos, pp. 215–242. Austin: University of Texas Press.

Ben-Amos, Paula. 1976. "A La Recherche du Temps Perdu": On Being an Ebony-Carver in Benin. In *Ethnic and Tourist Arts*, ed. Nelson A. Graburn, pp. 334–349. Berkeley: University of California Press.

Blakey, Michael. n.d. Racism Through the Looking Glass: An Afro-American Perspective. *World Archaeological Bulletin* 2:46–50.

Blewett, Mary. 1989. Machines, Workers, and Capitalists: The Interpretation of Textile Industrialization in New England Museums. In *History Museums in the United States*, eds. Warren Leon and Roy Rosenzweig, pp.262–293. Urbana: University of Illinois Press.

Bodnar, John. 1986. Symbols and Servants: Immigrant America and the Limits of Public History. *Journal of American History* 73:137–151.

Boorstin, Daniel J. 1973. *The Image*. New York: Atheneum.

Breen, T. H. 1989. *Imagining the Past: East Hampton Histories*. Addison-Wesley.

———. 1990 *Imagining the Past*. Addison-Wesley.

Britton, Robert A. 1979. The Image of the Third World in Tourism Marketing. *Annals of Tourism Research* 6:318–329.

Bruner, Edward M. 1986. Experience and Its Expressions. In *The Anthropology of Experience*, eds. Victor M. Turner and Edward M. Bruner, pp. 3–30. Urbana: University of Illinois Press.

Buck, Roy C. 1977a. Making Good Business Better: A Second Look at Staged Tourist Attractions. *Journal of Travel Research* 15:30–32.

———. 1977b. The Ubiquitous Tourist Brochure. *Annals of Tourism Research* 4:195–207.

Burgess, Jacqueline and Gold, John R. 1985. Chapter 1: Place, the Media and Popular Culture. In *Geography the Media and Popular Culture*, eds. Jacqueline Burgess and John R. Gold, pp. 1–32. London: Croom Helm.

Cannadine, David. 1983. The Context, Performance and Meaning of Ritual: The British Monarchy and the 'Invention of Tradition' c. 1820–1977. In *The Invention of Tradition*, eds. Eric Hobsbawm and Terrence Ranger, pp. 101–164. Cambridge: Cambridge University Press.

Cohen, Eric. 1972. Toward a Sociology of International Tourism. *Social Research* 39:164–182.

———. 1973. Nomads from Affluence: Notes on the Phenomenon of Drifter-Tourism. *International Journal of Comparative Sociology* 14:89–103.

———. 1974. Who is a Tourist?: A Conceptual Clarification. *The Sociological Review* 22:527–555.

———. 1979a. Rethinking the Sociology of Tourism. *Annals of Tourism Research* 6:18–35.

———. 1979b. A Phenomenology of Tourist Experiences. *Sociology* 13:179–201.

Countryman, Edward. 1986. John Ford's Drums Along the Mohawk: The Making of an American Myth. In *Presenting the Past: Essays on History and the Public*, eds. Susan Porter Benson, Stephen Brier, and Roy Rosenzweig, pp. 87–102. Philadelphia: Temple University Press.

Crouch, Steve. 1974. *Steinbeck Country*. Palo Alto: American West Publishing Company.

Culler, Jonathan. 1981. Semiotics of Tourism. *American Journal of Semiotics* 1:127–140.

Curtis, James R. 1981. The Boutiquing of Cannery Row. *Landscape* 25:44–48.

————. 1985. The Most Famous Fence in the World, Fact and Fiction in Mark Twain's Hannibal. *Landscape* 28:8–14.

Dégh, Linda. 1966. Approaches to Folklore Research Among Immigrant Groups. *Journal of American Folklore* 79:551–556.

————. 1977/78. Grape Harvest Festival of Strawberry Farmers: Folklore or Fake? *Ethnologia Europaea* 10:114–131.

Dorson, Richard M. 1982. The State of Folkloristics from an American Perspective. *Journal of the Folklore Institute.* 19:71–105.

Dorst, John D. 1989. *The Written Suburb.* Philadelphia: University of Pennsylvania Press.

Dundes, Alan. 1985. Nationalistic Inferiority Complexes and the Fabrication of Fakelore: A Reconsideration of Ossian, the Kinder und Hausmärchen, the Kalevala, and Paul Bunyan. *Journal of Folklore Research* 22:5–18.

Ehemann, Jane. 1977. What Kind of Place is Ireland: An Image Perceived through the American Media. *Journal of Travel Research* 16:28–30.

Engbeck, Joseph H., Jr. 1980. *State Parks of California.* Portland: Graphic Arts Center Publishing.

Evans, Nancy H. 1978. Tourism and Cross-cultural Communication. In *Tourism and Behavior,* ed. Valene L. Smith, pp. 41–53. Studies in Third World Societies Publication Number Five.

Evans-Prichard, Deirdre. 1987. The Portal Case: Authenticity, Tourism, Traditions, and the Law. *Journal of American Folklore* 100:276–296.

Fernandes, James W. 1986. *Persuasians and Performances.* Bloomington: Indiana University Press.

Fine, Elizabeth C. and Speer, Jean Haskell. 1985. Tour Guide Performances as Sight Sacralization. *Annals of Tourism Research* 12:73–95.

Finnegan, Ruth. 1969. Attitudes to the Study of Oral Literature in British Social Anthropology. *Man* 4:59–69.

Fleming, Ronald Lee. 1981. Recapturing History, A Plan for Gritty Cities. *Landscape* 25:20–27.

Ford, Larry R. 1984. The Burden of the Past, Rethinking Historic Preservation. *Landscape* 28:41–48.

Frisch, Michael H. 1986. The Memory of History. In *Presenting the Past: Essays on History and the Public,* eds. Susan Porter Benson, Stephen Brier, and Roy Rosenzweig, pp. 5–17. Philadelphia: Temple University Press.

————. 1989. The Presentation of Urban History in Big-City Museums. In *History Museums in the United States*, eds. Warren Leon and Roy Rosenzweig, pp.38–63. Urbana: University of Illinois Press.

————. 1990. *A Shared Authority*. Albany, New York: The State University of New York Press.

Gamper, Josef Adolf. 1981. Tourism in Austria, A Case Study of the Influence of Tourism on Ethnic Relations. *The Annals of Tourism Research* 8:432–446.

————. 1982. The Impact on Two Alpine Communities in Austria. Ph.D. dissertation, the University of California Berkeley.

Gordon, Ron. 1975. *Complete Guide to Monterey, Carmel, Big Sur*. Sun Valley, California: Monterey Guide.

Gossen, Gary H. 1972. Chamula Genres of Verbal Behavior. In *Towards New Perspectives in Folklore*, eds. Américo Paredes and Richard Bauman, pp. 145–168. Austin: University of Texas Press.

Gottlieb, Alma. 1982. Americans' Vacations. *Annals of Tourism Research* 9:165–187.

Graburn, Nelson. 1976. Introduction: Arts of the Fourth World. In *Ethnic and Tourist Arts*, ed. Nelson Graburn, pp. 2–32. Berkeley: University of California Press.

————. 1977. Tourism: The Sacred Journey. In *Hosts and Guests*, ed. Valene L. Smith, pp. 17–32. Philadelphia: University of Pennsylvania Press.

————. 1980. Teaching the Anthopology of Tourism. *International Social Science Journal* 32:56–68.

————, ed. 1983. *The Anthropology of Tourism*. New York: Pergammon Press.

————. 1984. The Evolution of Tourist Arts. *Annals of Tourism Research* 2:393–419.

Greenwood, Davydd J. 1977. Culture by the Pound: An Anthropological Perspective on Tourism as Cultural Commoditization. In *Hosts and Guests, the Anthropology of Tourism*, ed. Valene L. Smith, pp. 129–138. Philadelphia: University of Pennsylvania Press.

Hague, Harlan. 1983. The Reluctant Retirement of Thomas O. Larkin. *California History*. LXII:61–66.

Hall, Millicent. 1976. Theme Parks: Around the World in 80 Minutes. *Landscape* 21:3–8.

Handler, Richard. 1988. *Nationalism and the Politics of Culture in Québec.* Madison: University of Wisconsin Press.

Handsman, Russell G. 1980. Studying Myth and History in Modern America: Perspectives for the Past from the Continent. *Review in Anthropology* 7:255–268.

Heenan, David A. 1978. Tourism and the Community: A Drama in Three Acts. *Journal of Travel Research* 16:30–32.

Hemp, Michael. 1986. *Cannery Row, the History of Old Ocean View Avenue.* Monterey: The History Company.

Hicks, John and Regina. 1973. *Monterey, A Pictorial History.* Carmel, California: Creative Books.

Hobsbawm, Eric. 1983a. Introduction: Inventing Traditions. In *The Invention of Tradition,* eds. Eric Hobsbawm and Terrence Ranger, pp. 1–14. Cambridge: Cambridge University Press.

———. 1983b. Mass-Producing Traditions: Europe, 1870–1914. In *The Invention of Tradition,* eds. Eric Hobsbawm and Terrence Ranger, pp. 263–307. Cambridge: Cambridge University Press.

Holloway, J. Christopher. 1981. The Guided Tour, A Sociological Approach. *Annals of Tourism Research* 8:377–402.

Hosmer, Charles B., Jr. 1965. *Presence of the Past: A History of the Preservation Movement in the United States before Williamsburg.* New York: G.P. Putman's Sons.

Kirker, Harold. The Larkin House Revisited. *California History.* LXV:26–33, 73–74.

Kirshenblatt-Gimblett, Barbara. 1988. Mistaken Dichotomies. *Journal of American Folklore.* 101:140–155.

Kulik, Gary. 1989. Designing the Past. In *History Museums in the United States,* eds. Warren Leon and Roy Rosenzweig, pp. 2–37. Urbana: University of Illinois Press.

Langum, David J. 1983. From Condemnation to Praise, Shifting Perspectives on Hispanic California. *California History.* LXI:283–289,290.

Lears, T. J. Jackson. The Concept of Cultural Hegemony: Problems and Possibilities. *The American Historical Review.* 90:567–593.

Leon, Warren and Rosenzweig, Roy, eds. 1989. *History Museums in the United States.* Urbana: University of Illinois Press.

Leone, Mark. 1981. Archaeology's Relationship to the Present and the Past. In *Modern Material Culture, The Archaeology of Us,* eds. Richard A. Gould and Michael B. Schiffer, pp. 5–13. New York: Academic Press.

———. 1981a. The Relationship between Artifacts and the Public in Outdoor History Museums. *Annals of the New York Academy of the Sciences.* 376:301–314.

———. 1982. Childe's Offspring. In *Symbolic and Structural Archaeology,* ed. Ian Hodder, pp. 179–184. Cambridge: Cambridge University Press.

Lowenthal, David. 1985. *The Past is a Foreign Country.* Cambridge: Cambridge University Press.

McBryde, Isabel. ed. 1985. *Who Owns the Past? Papers from the Annual Symposium of the Australian Academy of the Humanities.* 1985. Oxford University Press.

MacCannell, Dean. 1973. Staged Authenticity: Arrangements of Social Space in Tourist Settings. *American Journal of Sociology* 79:589–603.

———. 1976. *The Tourist.* New York: Schocken Books.

———. 1979. Ethnosemiotics. *Semiotica* 27:149–171.

———. 1984. Reconstructed Ethnicity, Tourism and Cultural Identity in Third World Communities. *Annals of Tourism Research* 2:375–391.

Mangelsdorf, Tom. 1986. *A History of Steinbeck's Cannery Row.* Santa Cruz: Western Tanager Press.

Manning, Frank E. 1977. Cup Match and Carnival: Secular Rites of Revitalization in Decolonizing, Tourist-Oriented Societies. In *Secular Ritual,* eds. Sally F. Moore and Barbara G. Myerhoff, pp. 265–281. The Netherlands: Van Gorcum and Company.

Moore, Alexander. 1980. Walt Disney World: Bounded Ritual Space and the Playful Pilgrimage Center. *Anthropological Quarterly* 53:207–218.

Morin, Edgar. 1958. Tourism and Movies. *Landscape* 7:5.

Myerhoff, Barbara. 1986. Life Not Death in Venice: Its Second Life. In *The Anthropology of Experience,* eds. Victor W. Turner and Edward M. Bruner, pp. 261–286. Urbana: University of Illinois Press.

Neubert, Robert. 1981. Cannery Row, Life, Death and Resurrection. *Monterey Life* (Feb):62–71.

Nochlin, Linda. 1988. *Women, Art, and Power.* New York: Harper and Row.

Nuñez, Theron. 1977. Touristic Studies in Anthropological Perspective. In *Hosts and Guests,* ed. Valene L. Smith, pp. 207–216. Philadelphia: University of Pennsylvania Press.

Paredes, America and Bauman, Richard, eds. 1972. *Towards New Perspectives in Folklore.* Austin: University of Texas Press.

Parkington, John and Smith, Andrew B. 1986. Guest Editorial. *The South African Archaeological Bulletin* XLI:43–44.

Pearce, Douglas G. 1979. Towards a Geography of Tourism. *Annals of Tourism Research* 6:245–272.

Pearce, Philip L. and Moscardo, Gianno M. 1986a. The Concept of Authenticity in Tourist Experiences. *The Austrialian and New Zealand Journal of Sociology* 22:121–132.

———. 1986b. Historic Theme Parks. *The Annals of Tourism Research* 13:467–479.

Pi-Sunyar, Oriol. 1981. Tourism and Anthropology. *Annals of Tourism Research* 8:271–284.

Raymond, Henri. 1963–64. Utopia All-Inclusive. *Landscape* 13:4–7.

Redfield, Robert. 1947. The Folk Society. *American Journal of Sociology.* 52:293–308.

Reis, Elizabeth. Cannery Row, the AFL, the IWW, and Bay Area Italian Cannery Workers. *California History.* LXIV:174–191, 241–242.

Relph, Edward. 1976. *Place and Placelessness.* London: Pion Limited.

Ryan, Loretta Anne. 1987. Lowell in Transition: The Uses of History in Urban Change. Ph.D. dissertation, Columbia University.

Schickel, Richard. 1968. *The Disney Version.* New York: Avon Books.

Schlereth, Thomas, J. 1981. *Artifacts and the American Past.* American Association for State and Local History.

———, ed. *Material Culture Studies in America.* 1982. American Association for State and Local History.

———. *Cultural History and Material Culture: Everyday Life, Landscapes, Museums.* 1989. University of Michigan Research Press.

Schmidt, Catherine J. 1979. The Guided Tour, Insulated Adventure. *Urban Life* 7:441–467.

Sears, John F. 1982. Tourists in an Industrial Scene: Mauch Chunk, Pennsylvania. *Landscape* 26:1–9.

Smith, Valene, ed. 1977. *Hosts and Guests.* Philadelphia: University of Pennsylvania Press.

Stein, Jean. 1958. William Faulkner. In *Writers at Work,* ed. Malcolm Cowley, pp. 122–141. New York: The Viking Press.

Steinbeck, Elaine and Wallsten, Robert. 1975. *Steinbeck A Life in Letters.* New York: Viking Press.

Steinbeck, John. 1935. *Tortilla Flat.* New York: Random House.

————. 1945. *Cannery Row.* New York: Bantam Books.

————. 1954. *Sweet Thursday.* New York: Bantam Books.

Thompson, Michael. 1979. *Rubbish Theory.* Oxford: Oxford University Press.

Trilling, Lionel. 1971. *Sincerity and Authenticity.* Cambridge: Harvard University Press.

Turner, Victor W. and Bruner, Edward M., eds. 1986. *The Anthropology of Experience.* Urbana: University of Illinois Press.

Van den Berghe, Pierre L. and Keyes, Charles. 1984. Introduction, Tourism and Re-created Ethnicity. *Annals of Tourism Research* 2:343–352.

Wagner, Ulla. 1977. Out of Time and Place—Mass Tourism and Charter Trips. *Ethnos* 42:38–52.

Wallace, Michael. 1986. Visiting the Past, History Museums in the United States. In *Presenting the Past: Essays on History and the Public,* eds. Susan Porter Benson, Stephen Brier, and Roy Rosenzweig, pp. 137–161. Philadelphia: Temple University Press.

————. 1987. Industrial Museums and the History of Deindustrialization. *The Public Historian* 9:9–19.

————. 1989. Mickey Mouse History: Portraying the Past at Disney World. In *History Museums in the United States,* eds. Warren Leon and Roy Rosenzweig, pp. 158–180. Urbana: University of Illinois Press.

Weible, Robert. 1984. Lowell: Building a New Appreciation for Historical Place. *The Public Historian* 6:27–38.

Wollenberg, Charles. 1985. A Usable History for a Multicultural State. *California History* LXIV:203–209, 243–244.

Wright, Patrick. 1985. *On Living in an Old Country: The National Past in Contemporary Britain.* Routledge-Chapman & Hall.

Wylie, Alison. 1985. Putting Shakertown Back Together: Critical Theory in Archaeology. *Journal of Anthropological Archaeology* 4:133–147.

Zinsser, William. 1978. They Keep Mixin' Fact and Fiction in Hannibal, Mo. *Smithsonian* 9:155–161.

INDEX

❖   ❖   ❖   ❖   ❖

121

Printed in the United States
133587LV00007B/1-15/A